BARBARA TECHEL

I'm Fine Just the Way I Am

Healing *Emotional Pain* through the Wisdom of *Animals* and *Oracles*

Copyright © 2020 by Barbara Techel
All rights reserved.

While the incidents in this book did happen, some of the names of individuals and places have been changed. Any resulting resemblance to persons living or dead is entirely coincidental and unintentional.

No part of this book may be reproduced or transmitted in any form or by any means, electronic or mechanical, including photocopying, recording, or by any information storage and retrieval system without the written permission of the author, except where permitted by law.

Published in the United States by Joyful Paw Prints Press, LLC, Elkhart Lake, WI, www.joyfulpaws.com
Library of Congress Cataloging-in-Publication Data
2019917670

Editor: Dana Micheli
Cover photograph: Lisa A. Lehmann
Cover Design by 100Covers.com
Interior Design by FormattedBooks.com

ISBN: 978-09882499-5-0

To Gidget.
For the utmost love and loyalty as you guided me
to observe life sideways and reach far deeper and
expand far wider than I ever thought I could.

And the day came when the risk to remain tight in a bud was more painful than the risk it took to blossom.

—Anaïs Nin

Also By Barbara Techel

Memoirs
Through Frankie Eyes: One woman's journey to her authentic self and the dog on wheels who led the way
Wisdom Found in the Pause—Joie's Gift

Children's Books
Frankie the Walk 'N Roll Dog
Frankie the Walk 'N Roll Dog Visits Libby's House

WHAT PEOPLE ARE SAYING ABOUT I'M FINE JUST THE WAY I AM

Barbara's well written new book, I'm Fine Just the Way I Am, *takes you on a beautiful journey of self-awareness and self-discovery through the relationship she shares with her beloved dog, Gidget, a special needs dachshund. This inspirational memoir is sure to bring healing to all readers through Barbara's courage to stand in the light and in the dark, as Gidget's masterful teachings weave their way through her heart and soul.*

—Tammy Billups, author of *Soul Healing with Our Animal Companions,* and *Animal Soul Contracts*

Barbara's writing is bold, courageous, loving and necessary as a means to heal not only our own hearts, but the entire heart of the planet. I'm Fine Just the Way I Am *is a testament to the power of transparency and vulnerability, and how the human heart can be transformed over and over when we allow ourselves to fully live from love.*

—Sage Lewis, author of *Where Angels Play: Life, Death and the Magic Beyond* and *JAVA: The True Story of a Shelter Dog Who Rescued a Woman,* and producer of *Jungle Jaguar: Drum Journey Experience,* dancingporcupine.com

When we read another's struggle, oftentimes we can relate, encouraging us to reflect on our own inner workings. Barbara's book, I'm Fine Just the Way I Am *guides us through her self-discovery using the help of her animal companion, Gidget, along with other alternative methods which open the door to her sacred wisdom. We consider animals our pet, but Barbara shows us they are much more, taking on our illness, our anxiety, and our confusion, mirroring our issues so we can learn how to change. This concept is profoundly powerful.*

—Lynne Carol Austin, healer, artist, author of *Gull Soup*
and *Ten of Swords,* lynnecarolaustin.com

Barbara's words are from her deepest heart, they share her personal story along with the truth of living life authentically and connected to spirit. I value her words and writing enormously, they illuminate a path that I have walked for many years. But I value Barbara's honesty and her sweetness as she loves life and all that it holds. I'm Fine Just the Way I Am *is a must read for anyone seeking an inner connection and anyone who shares a love for animals and their powerful healing for each of us. It speaks the truth, in loving and very real ways. I know you will enjoy it!*

—Marggie Hatala, RN, BSN, Reiki Master, CEOLD,
author and reflective writing coach, marggiehatala.com

In this heartfelt, wise, honest, and tender book, Barbara offers a vision of hard-won healing and wisdom through the love of a special needs dog. It's an affirming message of hope and grace, reminding us of the tremendous teaching and love animals so generously offer.

—Elizabeth Hunter Diamond, professional clairvoyant
and energy healer, elizabethhunterdiamond.com

Barbara Techel recounts her insightful journey of surprising self-discovery, focusing on hope and healing. She shares the remarkable wisdom of the animal and human teachers who appeared when needed to help her recover from a deep childhood wound, making their wisdom accessible to all of us.

—Jenny Pavlovic, author of *8 State Hurricane Kate: The Journey and Legacy of a Katrina Cattle Dog*, and the *Not Without My Dog Resource & Record Book*

Barbara Techel's passionate love for dogs is evident in her words. She has a deep respect for the animal world and how they are masterful teachers and healers along our path. Her raw and touching story shows how our lives can be forever changed by their presence.

—Suzanne Hanna, founder and creator of
The Wilderness Walk and Global Healing Collective

CONTENTS

Introduction XIII

1	A Vision	1
2	Letting Go	5
3	The Niggle	10
4	Wait Until You See My Gidget	13
5	Obstacles	17
6	Welcoming Gidget	20
7	Heart Concerns	23
8	Seizures	29
9	Wheelchair Therapy	35
10	Unraveling	39
11	White Wolf Laiola	43
12	Feared Creature	48
13	Snake Ally	53
14	Ollie the Horse	57
15	Growing Angst	66
16	Judgment	71
17	Cycle of Confusion	74
18	Gidget Speaks	78
19	Kinship Connection	85

20	Personal Mastery	94
21	Second Chances	97
22	Reaching Out	102
23	Talking to Joe	107
24	Pet Caregiver Burden	113
25	Not Alone	117
26	The Choice	121
27	Surrendering	126
28	Getting Help	132
29	Following the Signs	141
30	Dreams	145
31	Gidget's Reflection	151
32	Grace Becoming	154
33	Animal and Oracle Wisdom	157
34	Out of the Shadows	161
35	No Place Like Home	167
36	Loyalty	170
37	Full Circle	173
38	Closure	176

Afterword	179
Acknowledgements	185
Resources	187
About the Author	189

INTRODUCTION

"I WANT TO let her go!"

With those six seemingly simple words, the intense searing sensation that had gripped my throat just moments before disappeared.

A bit surprised, I glanced around at the members of my monthly women's mastermind circle, then back to Pam, whose question had prompted those liberating words.

I'd just shared how I was struggling with whether or not to put my dog Gidget to sleep due to her chronic health challenges. I'd reached the end of my rope. I didn't know if I could do it anymore. I also wondered if it was fair to continue to put Gidget through this.

Pam had listened along with the others, then, in the most compassionate and caring voice, she asked, "What is it your heart really wants, Barb?"

My stomach knotted and I felt a painful lump form in my throat as I tried to find the words, and the courage, to express what felt so shameful. It was like I was in a dark cave and the walls were closing in around me.

"It's okay…" Pam said gently.

I felt a sudden urgency rising to release what I was feeling, yet I was still scared to do it. My heart beating wildly, I hugged the oversized pillow on my lap to my chest and rested my chin on its edge. It was then that I finally realized what I had been wanting to say but had been stifled by the guilt and shame: "I want to let her go."

Though my relief was immediate and palpable, I had no idea that the truth I'd just spoken would have such a deep, profound effect on my life. I had no idea that it was the beginning of a journey that would help me open to the parts inside of me that felt trapped, wounded, and constricted. These emotions had been building for far too many years, and though I didn't consciously realize it, I had been carrying them around like two tons of cement. Now it was time to let them go.

This was not a quick fix; nor did I take one specific path to the space of unprecedented freedom I experience today. What I do know is that it was the path, with all its twists and turns, that I was meant to travel.

Along the way I would come to realize that if we can find the courage to open our heart and trust that our pain has something to teach us, then letting go is like a dam. Once it bursts open, the fierce struggle we held onto loosens its grip and we can flow with more ease and peace.

One of the reasons I felt called to write this book is to help others shift and let go of their repressed or unaddressed pain. I once read somewhere, "No pain is greater or less, it is simply different." This struck a deep chord of resonance within me, as in speaking with women I often sense pain that for one reason or another they keep locked inside themselves.

While I have no doubt that this also happens with men, my experiences tell me that women are more commonly engaged in this endless inner battle. When left to fester, these feelings—be it guilt or shame, fear of judgment or rejection—tend to manifest in a variety of ways that we are often not consciously aware of and are certainly not for our highest good. They become our never-ending story that blocks us from becoming all we can be. On the other hand, if we learn to pay attention to the signals these emotions are sending us, and are willing to work with them, we can write a new story.

This is my journey to finally knowing that I'm *Fine Just the Way I Am*…

CHAPTER 1

A Vision

FOR OVER TWENTY years, dogs have played a pivotal role in my life, guiding me to expand and evolve.

It was June 21, 2017, five years after the death of my disabled dachshund, Frankie, that I was able to finally let her fully go. What was left of her was contained in a small plastic bag nestled in a chocolate brown wooden box. Her name was engraved on a gold plate affixed to the top.

As I held her ashes, my hands trembled slightly, though on a deeper level I understood that what I held wasn't really her. The real Frankie was part of the mystery of life, the vast cosmos we know as the Universe, God, Source, Divine, Creator, or Spirit. Her form, physical or ashes, didn't matter, for her spirit would live on forever.

In my first memoir, *Through Frankie's Eyes—One woman's journey to her authentic self and the dog on wheels who led the way*, I shared the many lessons I learned from Frankie. I also shared how my chocolate Lab, Cassie Jo, after being diagnosed with terminal bone cancer, helped me to begin to live more in the present.

As I observed Cassie Jo living each day so full of joy, it seemed to me she wasn't aware that she was going to die. This caused a shift in my awareness. I began pondering how I often lived in the past, wishing I could change things, or worrying about the future, which I could neither predict nor control. It was a rare occasion, I realized, when I truly savored the joy of living in the moment.

Nine months after Cassie Jo's passing, Frankie, who was six years old at the time, became paralyzed. The diagnoses—Intervertebral Disc Disease (IVDD)—meant that she'd live out her life in a wheelchair made for dogs. It also meant a big change in my lifestyle. I had to learn the ins and outs of caring for a disabled dog, which, since the paralysis had left her incontinent, included expressing her bladder. While I resisted and struggled at the beginning, it was Frankie who helped me to see my challenges in a positive way, rather than getting stuck in the negative.

She also helped me to begin to let go of worrying what others thought of me and my choices. I became fascinated by this ten-inch-tall dog who, despite being in a wheelchair, just got on with the business of being a dog. Frankie didn't care what others thought, and by observing her, it occurred to me that maybe I didn't have to care so much either. I was beginning to build a new sense of confidence in myself; I was beginning to find my voice and feel more comfortable about using it.

I still recall with a smile how Frankie didn't even know she had wheels. She carried on doing most things as she'd done before—going for walks, sitting in the sun, cuddling, napping, and playing with our new Lab puppy Kylie, who we brought home five months after Cassie Jo passed away.

It was on a warm morning in June, the day before the fifth anniversary of Frankie's passing, that she came to me while I was in meditation. Feeling compelled to share this experience, I wrote about it on my blog:

> *I didn't start out to be with you, sitting alone on the beach staring out at the ocean. But then out of the corner of my eye, I saw you rolling toward me, your ears blowing in the wind.*
>
> *I was so happy to see you! I scooped you up, and gently placed you in my lap. We sat silently letting the water lull us dreamily into another realm as waves lapped softly onto my feet, and my wide-brimmed straw hat shaded your sweet face.*
>
> *The feel of your silky fur against my arms and your heart beating with mine moved me to tears as they slid slowly down my cheeks.*

I heard Frankie say, "It's okay."

Knowing she understood my deepest thoughts and emotions I knew we were connecting in this most magical moment.

"Those ashes in the box lovingly resting on the shelf are not me," she said. "They're what's left of my physical body. Who I really am is alive and well in spirit.

You aren't letting go, but instead releasing me back to where it is I came from.

And that is with the stars and universe, safely and lovingly residing with our creator.

A place you can join me whenever you choose is in your thoughts or heart until we meet again on the other side.

But you see I've been preparing you for this day. I've watched you grow stronger with each passing year. And you now understand that I never left you. We have always been connected in our hearts.

Letting go of what is left of the physical of my ashes will not change that, but only deepen what is true."

In the innermost part of my being, I understood everything she was conveying to me. And I knew I was indeed okay.

I was ready more than ever for this final sacred step.

To release her, with trust and faith, and a knowing in my heart, that this was the right thing to do.

"Let's walk," I heard her say.

Strolling together along the shore I marveled at her sweet, wise self, rolling beside me.

There were no more words or thoughts to be exchanged. We just simply were. We had come to an understanding. My heart felt a full circle of healing.

Just as she had come to me in this space of meditation, I saw myself stand still, as she continued on without me, rolling down the sandy shore on her own, fading into the light from which she came.

I stood for a moment in sincere gratitude and then turned to walk back down the beach. While I was once again alone with my thoughts, I now felt more at peace in this new space of awareness that I am indeed *never alone. For all the magical, loving, blessed moments I had with my dear sweet, Frankie, she will always be a part of me.*

That meditation was the Universe's way of telling me it was time to give her back completely to the place from which she had come.

CHAPTER 2

Letting Go

THE NEXT MORNING I was awakened by the five-a.m. sun streaming through the blinds. I tried to go back to sleep, but it was no use. It was the fifth anniversary of Frankie's death, and after the vision I had received in my meditation the day before, I knew it was time to release her ashes.

I lay in bed a bit longer thinking about her, and it occurred to me that in August she would have been seventeen years old. This was a significant marker.

Five years and one day earlier, before I made the decision to help Frankie cross to the other side, I'd had a reading by animal communicator, Dawn Brunke. I remembered telling Dawn how I wished Frankie could have lived to be seventeen, though I didn't really know why I thought that. Dawn shared that Frankie *felt* seventeen—meaning she had lived a full life and was ready to move on. That was comforting for me to hear. Now, I couldn't help but link the significance of that with my being ready to scatter her ashes.

I hadn't made any specific plans for how I would release Frankie's remains. All I knew was that I wanted to scatter her ashes around my writing cottage. I also wanted to trust and follow the flow of my heart and let it be my guide.

A half hour later I climbed out of bed. I did my usual routine of feeding my dogs, Gidget and Kylie, and put the kettle on to boil water for tea. I then made my way out to my writing cottage, a quaint ten-by-twelve space located off the end of my deck and twelve steps from my bedroom patio doors. When I first began writing I would just pull up a chair at the kitchen table. But soon I realized I wanted a space of my own, and in the summer of 2009, I brought up the idea to my husband John. I sold a car I loved to pay for most of the materials and John, a carpenter by trade, built me the cottage as a labor of love.

The outside of the cottage is olive green with a Victorian screen door and scroll detail painted periwinkle—my favorite color. The inside is painted a light periwinkle, has a petite gas stove to keep me warm in the winter and a small air conditioner to cool me in the summer. With seven windows, it lets in plenty of natural light. It has changed over the years, but currently contains a desk for writing, a table to work on art projects, a table where I do my oracle readings and a chair for meditation, reading or contemplation. Most days I also roll out a mat and do my yoga practice there.

I had evolved in so many ways within these four walls over the years, so though my heart felt heavy at the thought, it also felt right for this to be Frankie's final resting place.

I lit a candle and felt called to pull a card from my deck of SoulCollage® cards. SoulCollage is a creative and reflective process, created by Seena Frost, in which I had been trained as a facilitator in 2014. The process entails working with images from magazines, collaging them onto 5 x 8 cardstock, and then intuitively consulting with them for guidance and wisdom.

The card I pulled—one I had made during the winter solstice two years before—resonated deeply with me. The solstice meant the days would now become longer and lighter, and the card, which included a picture of Frankie, reminded me of her greatest gift—she had taught me to look for the light in dark times and to also be the light as an example for others.

At first, I didn't know whether I'd blog about my experience releasing Frankie's ashes; I just decided to follow my intuition in creating a ritual that felt right to me. I eventually realized I'd write about it as a way of capturing this sacred moment and in bringing my story with Frankie to completion.

All the memories of Frankie came flooding back as I sat in my oversized floral wicker chair in my writing cottage, holding her ashes in my hands. I thought about how often she had lain in her bed on this very chair as I followed my desire to capture my thoughts and feelings through my blog, two children's books, and a memoir about her.

She had been among the stars for some time now, yet I had continued to hold onto her ashes as if that would keep her close to me. Now I finally understood she would always be a part of me, even though she was no longer in the small, long body I could physically hold and hug.

Frankie had taught me so much about the joy of living. She also taught me that death need not be feared. She helped me to trust and know that our spirit lives on and that we can connect with our crossed-over loved ones whenever we want.

Oracle cards are another tool I use to help me connect with my inner wisdom. I've been fascinated with this ancient practice for many years now. They serve as inspiration, contemplation, or a jumping off point to help me go even deeper, acting as a reflection of what may be going on in my inner world that I can't always see.

During this sacred time with Frankie's ashes, I also felt called to pull two oracle cards. I pulled one card from the *Power Animal Oracle Cards* by Dr. Steven Farmer and received Dragonfly. I then pulled a card from the *Soul Coaching Oracle Deck* by Denise Linn and received Joy.

Again, the cards were in perfect resonance with the ritual I was doing in Frankie's honor. Frankie had definitely brought joy, not only into my life, but to the thousands of kids and adults she had inspired while she was alive. To this day I still hear from people who read my books and were encouraged by Frankie's resilience and buoyancy of spirit.

The words on the front of the Dragonfly card—"You know who you are"—were profound as well. I had indeed become so much more of who I am because of Frankie. Though I was still growing and evolving, my experiences with Frankie had made me more confident about sharing myself with the world.

As I looked at the Dragonfly and Joy cards side-by-side, I realized they were telling me that it was now time for Frankie to fly free, and in this, I could find joy. It didn't have to be sad, but a celebration of our beautiful relationship.

I smiled through my tears.

Continuing to follow my intuition, I rolled out my yoga mat. As I moved through various poses, a thought came to me to sit with the box of Frankie's ashes when I was done with my practice, and listen to the song "Landslide" by Stevie Nicks.

For those of you unfamiliar with the song, it is about the difficulty of embracing change. It can be frightening to have things fall away, usually because we don't realize that within the change are unexpected gifts that will help us understand and grow deeper in our wisdom. Whenever I heard "Landslide" my thoughts always automatically went to Frankie. The work we'd done together—visiting schools and libraries, and as a therapy dog team going to hospitals, hospice and nursing homes—was incredibly rewarding, and it was not easy to let it, or her, go. The words to the song perfectly expressed the fear of change I felt.

Indeed, it was this song that was playing as I sat on the deck one afternoon two weeks after Frankie's passing. I was thinking about her when a hummingbird hovered for several moments inches from my face. I had no doubt it was Frankie letting me know she was okay. I wrote about this experience in my book, *Through Frankie's Eyes*.

As the song suggests, time had made me stronger and bolder. Getting older has undoubtedly brought me to a new place of understanding about why I'm here on earth, and Frankie had played a key part in that journey as well.

I don't believe we "get over" a loss, but what I've often shared with others seeking comfort after the death of a pet is to be gentle and allow themselves to move *through* grief.

I've also come to understand that grief is something we live *with*. Meaning, it becomes a part of who we are. It changes us. We aren't the same as before. And hopefully we can rest in a deeper place of peace and a knowing that to love so profoundly means we also get to experience great joy.

With Frankie's box of ashes on my lap, I remembered when I took them off the shelf the day before and heard a rattling inside. I wasn't sure what it was and decided to wait until I was ready to open it this morning.

The sun was streaming through the window, warming my face as I took a deep breath and opened the box. I smiled when I saw the source of the rattling. It was the flat stone upon which I'd written Frankie's name and the dates of her birth and death.

I gently removed the plastic bag containing her ashes and held them in my hands and I realized I was holding my breath. As I exhaled, I knew it was time to take this final step of letting go. Though I felt some resistance, I reminded myself again that this wasn't really Frankie I was holding. Her spirit was alive and well and always would be.

I slowly walked the few feet across my writing cottage, pushed open the screen door, walked across the deck, and down the stairs onto the lawn. The stillness of the morning was deeply moving; it felt as if mother earth was tenderly holding me during this sacred time.

I reached inside the plastic bag and felt the roughness of the ashes. My hands shook slightly and my legs felt a bit wobbly, yet something guided me as I scooped out a portion of Frankie's ashes and began to sprinkle them on the ground. Step by sacred step I moved around my writing cottage, releasing Frankie back to the earth.

As I made my way to the east side, the honeysuckle I had planted in Frankie's memory came into view. I knew immediately what I was going to do. My heart smiled as I released the last of her ashes around the base of the plant, making her one with it.

When I was done, I stood for a few moments staring at the ground where Frankie's ashes lay. I then recalled hearing earlier that morning that rain was expected later in the day. It comforted me to know this would help to soak Frankie's ashes deeper into the earth.

Once back inside my writing cottage, I sat quietly for a little while longer, shedding a few tears, yes, but mostly filled with gratitude that the morning had flowed just as it was meant to. I felt at peace.

CHAPTER 3

The Niggle

RELEASING FRANKIE'S ASHES was a turning point that allowed me to do the same with the ashes of my second disabled dachshund, Joie (pronounced Joey). While my dogs to that point had taught me valuable lessons while they were alive, Joie's true teaching would reveal itself to me only after she had passed.

I had adopted Joie from a rescue in Washington State in the fall of 2012, four months after Frankie died. Like Frankie, she had IVDD and was paralyzed in her hind limbs. Unfortunately, Joie was only with me for ten short months before I had to say goodbye to her. Unbeknownst to me she had numerous health complications in addition to the IVDD, which were discovered when she had a CT scan to confirm a moderate tear in her neck. After much soul-searching, I had made the humane decision to euthanize her in August of 2013.

Before I knew it, four years had passed and in August 2017 I found myself scattering Joie's ashes in the gardens around my writing cottage so she could join Frankie. Later, it occurred to me that after Cassie Jo passed, John and I hadn't waited that long to scatter her ashes, though we had done it separately. He took part of Cassie Jo's ashes to a park they visited most

Sundays to play ball. I scattered the remainder of her ashes under the maple tree in our front yard where she loved to relax.

Why, I now wondered, had it taken me this long to do the same with Frankie and Joie's ashes? I realized it was because I couldn't let go, not just of my beloved companions, but of the identity I had created for myself. More recently, I had been feeling the need to move in a new direction, but fear and the question of who I was without Frankie or Joie had stopped me from doing so.

Since retiring Frankie in early 2012, I had heard an inner whisper to slow down. For five years we had been on a mission, one that had kept me especially busy, and though I would not change a thing about this beautiful and pivotal time in my life, I was exhausted.

Yet, I continued to ignore that inner voice. Just the idea of taking a step back from my work was scary, for through it I thought I'd found my purpose. *Who was I without it?* I wondered, *Was this it? Was my purpose complete?* These disconcerting questions ran endlessly through my mind, and when I adopted Joie I thought perhaps I would continue the same work and mission, this time with her as my partner. But it wasn't meant to be.

When I said goodbye to Joie it was difficult to accept that this was yet another nudge from Spirit and an opportunity for me to slow down. I contemplated taking a three-month sabbatical, but I kept fighting it. I didn't know how to do *nothing*. I also worried what others might think. In a society that glorifies busy-ness, would I be judged as lazy?

I recalled the beginning of this journey, the publication of my first children's book, and how uncomfortable I was with the attention it brought. I had grown up painfully shy, and while over the years I had learned to be more outgoing when I needed to be, my true essence remained that of a homebody and someone who needs quite a bit of quiet time. The idea of putting myself out in the world as a writer and, eventually, a speaker, seemed unthinkable, yet there I was, doing it.

Then word spread, and I found myself not only visiting schools and libraries but being interviewed on TV, radio and podcasts. Though it was quite unsettling, I was driven by the need to spread a positive message about dogs in wheelchairs and to educate others that these dogs can lead quality lives. Frankie was in a sense my security blanket, and once I realized it was usually her people wanted to meet, I began to relax and learn to embrace being in the public eye.

It had been a six-year whirlwind, and by the time Joie passed everything inside of me knew I had to take a break. This was further confirmed after speaking with Dan Blank, a mentor of mine who works with other creatives. Still, I was scared, as it meant I'd have to press pause on the activities that had become such a big part of my life—maintaining my blog, interaction on social media, and marketing my work. I also decided I would not consider bringing another dog into my life. This was a time to set aside any thoughts of what was next and go inward and just be for a while. I would eventually write about what I learned during that time in a second memoir, *Wisdom Found in the Pause—Joie's Gift.*

The sabbatical was certainly uncomfortable in the beginning. The first two weeks I was so restless I thought I'd jump out of my skin, but eventually I settled into a rhythm of calm and peace. While I still had my nervous and anxious moments, I was learning to be okay without an agenda and to just go with the flow of each day.

As for the thoughts of another dog, well, that proved to be a bit more challenging.

CHAPTER 4

Wait Until You See My Gidget

WHEN IN AUGUST of 2013 I decided to take a sabbatical, I didn't commit to a set length of time, probably because the idea of being away from my work so long was unnerving. However, when the end of September rolled around I felt I needed one more month. This worked out nicely, as John and I had planned a vacation to Asheville, North Carolina in October.

While I had faithfully traded writing and posting for inner reflecting and an easier pace, I had not been so successful in keeping my yearning for a new dog at bay. It continued to tickle my thoughts and tug at my heart. I wanted another dachshund with IVDD and in a wheelchair; or, perhaps one that was in need of a wheelchair which I could provide. This time, though, something felt different. I realized I didn't want to share this dog with others like I'd done with Frankie and attempted to with Joie. I wanted this dog all to myself.

At first, John wasn't on board with getting another dog, which didn't surprise me. It had been the same when we adopted our previous dachshunds, though once they were living with us, he grew to love them, often relishing in cuddling and playing with them. He also wasn't all that comfortable when Frankie and I began gaining attention from the book I'd published about her. He was worried it would take me away from home and that our life might change. But eventually he grew proud of the work Frankie and I were doing and supported me wholeheartedly.

John is a General Contractor, remodeling and building new homes. Imagine his surprise when while meeting with potential clients they would ask if he was related to me. When he told them I was his wife, they would excitedly exclaim, "You mean you are Frankie's Dad?!" It began to happen so often that we started to joke that Frankie was the reason he'd gotten the job!

There were many beautiful experiences about having a dog with special needs, though it did also mean restrictions on our freedom. It's challenging to find someone to care for a dog who needs their bladder and bowels expressed, which limits the amount of time you can be away from home. If you wish to get away for an extended period, taking your disabled dog on vacation is usually the only option. One can certainly understand that this isn't for everyone.

As I gave more thought to bringing yet another paralyzed pup into our life there was a part of me that felt guilty. I knew in my heart that if John had his way we wouldn't have another one. Yet I couldn't deny that taking care of a special needs dog fulfilled me in a way that nothing else seemed to do.

After an admittedly short tug of war between mind and heart, my heart won out and I began searching the internet for another paralyzed doxie. I didn't tell John I was looking. I knew I'd eventually have to tell him and I hoped and prayed he would be okay with it.

Fourteen days before we were to leave on vacation, I found my next dachshund on Petfinder.com. Her name was Gidget, and she was quite unusual looking, with gray, white and brown fur that bore a pattern of markings known as dapple. At only ten pounds, she was also tinier than my previous doxies. What drew me most, however, was her wise, sweet petite face.

I then clicked on the video footage shot by the rescue organization and was immediately smitten with her quirky, spunky and charismatic personality. It came shining through in the short film! From what I could tell, it appeared that Gidget did not need a wheelchair; instead, she had this endearing wobbly walk. I wasn't sure how I felt about that, as I was hoping to put good use to the wheelchair that had been Frankie's and then Joie's. Then again, it really didn't matter, because I was already head over heels in love.

I knew from experience that I was feeling the same heart connection with Gidget that I had shared with Frankie and Joie. But what to do? The timing wasn't right. We were going to be gone for ten days. Having walked this journey before, I knew the key lay in trusting that if something is meant to be it will happen. That isn't always easy, of course, and as we prepared for our departure to Asheville I prayed that Gidget would still be available in ten days.

I also decided to hold off on sharing the news with John. I had a pretty good idea what his initial reaction would be and I didn't want it to be on his mind during our vacation. I'd have plenty of time to get him used to the idea when we returned to Wisconsin.

While away, I tried hard to not check Gidget's page on PetFinder.com, but I couldn't help myself. Each time I looked and saw she was still there, my heart skipped a beat and hope stayed alive that all would turn out in my favor.

Our time in Asheville was filled with fun and laughter and taking in many delightful sites and delicious places to eat. But Gidget was never far from my thoughts, and by our last day there I couldn't wait any longer. I just had to tell John about Gidget.

He was sitting at the kitchen table inside the quaint, Swiss Chalet-style cabin we had rented in the mountains, scrolling through Facebook on my laptop. I knew it was now or never.

I said, "Can I show you something really adorable?"

"Sure."

I had bookmarked the video of Gidget, so it was easy to access. It opened with cue music—*Wait 'til You See My Gidget* by Johnny Tillotson—then Gidget flashed across the screen. She was being held in someone's arms, and her head was cocked to the side while she also leaned back, causing her ears to fly up over her head. Then the scene switched to her on someone else's lap and stretched out on her back as she enjoyed a belly rub. As the rest of the video played I couldn't help but think that Tillotson's song had been written just for her, as her tiny, quirky and sweet self was genuinely a *Gidget*!

When the video finished playing I was relieved to see that John was smiling. He looked at me and said, "So is she the one?"

"Well, I hope so. I haven't contacted the rescue yet. I decided to wait and trust that if she is meant to be ours she will still be available when we get back home."

Now that I had John's blessing, I could hardly contain my excitement as we drove back to Wisconsin. We'd barely set foot in our house when I sat down on the sofa in the living room and typed an email to the owner of the rescue to express my interest in adopting Gidget.

CHAPTER 5

Obstacles

ADOPTING JOIE FROM the rescue had been remarkably smooth, involving some paperwork and a short flight from Washington State to Wisconsin. Bringing Gidget into our lives would be a markedly different experience, however, one with many hurdles.

From my initial communications with Cheryl, the head of the rescue, I learned that Gidget had made her way to the organization after being surrendered to a shelter. The woman who relinquished Gidget was what Cheryl referred to as a "pretty dog collector." When I told her I'd never heard the term before, Cheryl explained that it's someone who gets a dog solely based on its looks.

It was the "pretty dog collector's" daughter who finally convinced her to surrender Gidget, now six years old, because she was unable to walk. While there wasn't a definitive diagnosis of IVDD, this was likely the cause of her immobility, as one in four dachshunds are afflicted with the disease.

In the weeks leading up to her adoption, I was a wreck. I already knew from Gidget's pictures and videos that she was quite the charmer and a love bug, and I grew concerned that Cheryl was going to change her mind about letting her go. When things weren't progressing as I'd hoped, I wrestled with feelings of frustration and even wondered at times why Gidget had been listed on PetFinder in the first place.

It took persistence and reaching out often to Cheryl to assure her I was seriously interested in having Gidget as part of my family. Though I feared this would end with a broken heart for me, I did my best to understand that Cheryl loved Gidget too and wanted what was best for her. This period of limbo made me think of people who wish to adopt a child and what they must go through when the birth mother changes her mind. If they could endure that kind of disappointment, I told myself, then I too could find a way to be at peace, no matter how things worked out with Gidget.

From my discussions with Cheryl it wasn't quite clear to me whether Gidget would need a wheelchair or not. One scene of the video shared on PetFinder showed her walking with the aid of a dog sling, while another showed her walking on her own with that endearing wobbly gait. It was evident from the video that Cheryl and her team of volunteers were instrumental in getting Gidget to be as mobile as she was. Judging from my experience, though, I thought perhaps a wheelchair might help strengthen Gidget's muscle tone and help her to walk even better than she currently was. I also, as mentioned earlier, wanted a doxie who needed a wheelchair so the one I had could be of use to another, but by this point I was okay with knowing that Gidget might be able to get along without it.

The other obstacle was that Gidget wasn't spayed. The procedure had been attempted, along with a dental cleaning, while she was under Cheryl's care, but Gidget almost died on the table. The dental work was completed, the spaying wasn't.

Part of my verbal agreement with Cheryl was that I not spay her. She said Gidget had a weak heart and felt it was too great of a risk to put her under anesthesia again.

I was somewhat apprehensive about this, as I had never had a dog that went into heat. Then again, I'd had to learn so much about caring for my previous dachshunds and I had done things I had never thought I'd be able to do. I would learn to tackle this too. No big deal.

Cheryl also shared with me that Gidget had been adopted once before but was surrendered back when the woman said Gidget was too much to handle. I knew that when a dog who has been paralyzed because of IVDD regains their mobility, their bladder and bowel function usually does not return. This means they need to be expressed several times a day to avoid leakage and poop accidents. At times this can feel overwhelming, and it does limit your life in terms of scheduling and being away from home on any given day. This, however, didn't give me pause. I had done it for both Frankie and Joie, so I was used to it. I also worked from home, so I would be able to accommodate Gidget's needs.

Despite our frequent communications, the adoption process continued to lag. I told Cheryl I was willing to fly to the West Coast to pick up Gidget, but it wasn't the expense she was concerned with. She needed to feel completely comfortable with my adopting Gidget, and that Gidget and I felt comfortable with each other. Finally, it was decided that Cheryl would fly Gidget to me. I would pick them up at the airport and take them to the hotel. Once there, Gidget and I could get to know each other, and if Cheryl felt it was a good fit she would fly back home the next day.

CHAPTER 6

Welcoming Gidget

IT WAS A cold and cloudy mid-November afternoon with snow flurries floating through the air when I drove to the airport. Cheryl's flight was due to arrive early evening—not an ideal time. I had concerns about driving back home after dark through the big and busy city of Milwaukee. I also wasn't one who enjoyed being up late.

But when I finally saw Cheryl walking down the terminal with Gidget in her arms, my heart flipped and melted all at the same time! I'd made a colorful poster-sized sign that read "Welcome Home, Gidget," which I held out so Cheryl could easily see me.

As Cheryl walked toward me with my next dachshund to love and care for it seemed like I was watching a movie in slow motion. I couldn't wait to hold Gidget! When we stood face to face Cheryl immediately held Gidget out to me and, as I felt the familiar sensation of my heart expanding to twice its size. There is just nothing like it!

With Gidget now in my arms, Cheryl and I quickly walked through the airport out to my car. We had an hour's drive to the hotel where Cheryl was staying and where Gidget and I could get to know each other better. I didn't want to waste a minute.

Once we arrived and were settled into Cheryl's room, she announced she was hungry.

"I'm going to see if the kitchen is still open," she said, "I won't be gone long. It will give you two some time to get acquainted."

Before she left, she bent down and handed Gidget a chew stick.

"These are her favorite."

Gidget held her head high and with her endearing wobbly walk, she promptly marched off to the bedroom to enjoy her treat.

When Cheryl closed the door behind her, I walked into the bedroom to be with Gidget. I wanted more than anything to hold and snuggle her in my arms, but she was far more interested in the chew stick. I couldn't blame her, really; she had been left alone with a stranger and besides, it's hard for anyone to compete with a chew stick.

As I watched her, I recalled our arrival at the hotel a few minutes earlier. When I drove up to the entrance so Cheryl could run inside to check in and get her room key, Gidget had whimpered with concern and stared intently through the car window after her. She seemed quite anxious, and a small worry flickered across my mind that she may have a hard time leaving Cheryl. Now my concern faded a bit, as Gidget was happily chomping on her treat and seemingly oblivious to the fact that Cheryl had left the room.

When Cheryl returned a few moments later she picked Gidget up and brought her into the living room. At first Gidget didn't have an interest in me and stayed at a distance. But eventually she began to warm up to me as I softly talked to her. Before I knew it, she was next to me, and then she was willing to sit on my lap. I couldn't get over how tiny she was, with such a petite frame and weighing only ten pounds.

My last two dachshunds were fourteen and twelve pounds, and I remembered thinking how I never wanted a dog smaller than them. Now, though, as I held Gidget in my arms, I was enjoying the fact she was lighter in weight and smaller in stature. I also realized that expressing her bladder and bowels, which I had done over the toilet with my first two doxies, would be easier on my back.

After about an hour, I was ready to head for home. But I also wanted to be respectful and honor Cheryl's need to feel comfortable that Gidget and I were a good match. Another hour passed, and by ten-thirty I was not only tired but concerned that John would be worried. After dropping a few hints that I was ready to leave, I was finally able to sign the adoption papers.

Cheryl and I had never agreed on an adoption fee for Gidget; she left it open for me to pay what I felt was fair. I also wanted to compensate her for the cost of the flight and hotel room, but she was adamant that I didn't need to. She told me a friend had taken care of it.

A price tag can never be put on love, but I had already decided on an amount a few days early, one that I felt expressed my gratitude that Cheryl had taken time away from her home and her husband to bring Gidget to me. When I handed her an envelope with five hundred dollars in it Cheryl objected, saying it was too much, but I was insistent that this felt right to me.

Finally she accepted, and I scooped Gidget into my arms so we could make our exit. Cheryl snapped a photo of me and Gidget together, then she walked out with us. As we reached my car, I couldn't help but notice the highway next to the hotel was buzzing with traffic. Though I was nervous about driving in the dark, I was excited to have Gidget as my co-pilot. I handed Gidget to Cheryl, opened the back door of my car, took out the dog car seat I'd brought along, and strapped it into the front passenger seat.

As I turned to take Gidget from Cheryl's arms I saw tears streaming down her face. I don't recall what was said, because my heart ached for her; I also had a moment of panic that she might change her mind at the last minute.

Instead, Cheryl handed Gidget back to me and I placed her in the dog seat and covered her with a blanket to keep her warm. I stepped aside as Cheryl leaned into the front seat and kissed the side of Gidget's face.

"You be good for Miss Barbara," she said sadly.

The tears were still flowing freely as she stepped back and closed the door. I could feel her sorrow and thought, not for the first time, that I could never be in the business of finding dogs new homes. The thought of getting attached and falling in love, only to say goodbye, seemed unbearable to me. I honestly don't know how those in rescue do this work, but I am sure thankful they do.

I gave Cheryl a hug and thanked her one last time, then got into the car. As I drove down and around the winding drive then out the hotel parking lot, Gidget stared out the back window and whimpered. This tore at my heart. I prayed she didn't feel Cheryl had abandoned her and that in time she would come to trust me and feel welcome in our home.

CHAPTER 7

Heart Concerns

FOR THE MOST part, Gidget settled in pretty quickly. She was clearly a snuggle bug and loved to be on my lap or beside me when I read or watched a program. But she also got anxious whenever I left the house. I sensed that if she had it her way, she would have gone with me everywhere. But that wasn't always possible.

When I did leave I put her in a kennel, and I'd often return to find she had chewed on her blanket, leaving tiny holes in it. Sometimes I'd find the blanket in shreds. I was concerned she may be having separation anxiety. As I had done in the past when facing challenges with my dogs, I reached out to Dawn, the animal communicator, to set up an appointment and find out how I could best help Gidget.

Dawn suggested I sit with Gidget for about fifteen minutes before I planned to leave home. She also said it was a good idea to talk directly with her, letting her know my plans and when I would return. It was also important to align my energy by remaining calm as this would help Gidget do the same.

Things improved and Gidget's anxiety seemed to lessen, but she still had her moments. I was also apprehensive about leaving Gidget to roam our house freely and potentially get into something and harm herself. Our Lab Kylie often rested in her kennel when we left home. We'd even taken the front door off of it because that was her happy place while we were gone. But I wasn't sure if it was a good idea to have them both roaming free until they got to know one another better. Kylie had always been the gentlest creature with my other dachshunds, but I didn't yet know Gidget's temperament well enough.

Two weeks later I took Gidget to my veterinarian, Dr. Benner, for a thorough examination. I didn't have much of a health record for her, but I did know she'd had urinary tract infections in the past—which was evidence of IVDD—that she almost died during surgery, and that she'd be going into heat at some point. I also told him that Cheryl believed Gidget had a weak heart and that it would be too risky to put her under anesthesia again.

After I shared what I knew about Gidget and her circumstances, he placed his stethoscope on her chest and listened to her heart.

After a few moments, he said, "I don't think there's anything wrong with Gidget's heart."

"Are you sure?" I said.

"Yes. I do detect a murmur (I don't recall the exact name of it now) but it's a common murmur found in dogs. Many of my patients have it. It's nothing to be concerned with and shouldn't affect her while under anesthesia."

I wanted to believe this was indeed the case, but I found it difficult to dismiss what Cheryl had said to me. Dr. Benner said that not spaying Gidget increased her risk of pyometra—an infection and inflammatory disorder of the uterus typically occurring in female dogs that haven't been spayed. Because it often goes undetected until it's too late, it can cause a painful death. He also said she had a higher risk of developing mammary tumors.

"Quite honestly, the risk of her developing pyometra is much higher than the risk of putting her under anesthesia."

I found myself torn as I struggled to make sense of this conflicting information. On one hand, there was the risk of pyometra, which I'd never heard of until now. On the other hand, I was still worried about the previous health information I'd been given, plus the agreement I'd made with Cheryl that I would not spay Gidget. I wanted to do the right thing for her, but both choices seemed to carry enormous risks.

Finally, Dr. Benner said, "Let me ask another vet to come in and listen to her heart."

Relieved, I said, "That would be great. Thank you."

A few moments later Dr. Benner came back into the room with Dr. Penny. She took a few moments to listen to Gidget's heart and concurred with Dr. Benner that there was a murmur but it was common and nothing to be concerned about.

I thanked Dr. Penny, but while I appreciated the second opinion I was still hesitant.

"Why would the woman from the rescue tell me this about her heart if it isn't true?" I asked.

"I don't know," Dr. Brenner replied, "though I will be honest with you and tell you I've heard many different rescue stories over the years that don't always make sense."

He then suggested that if it would help put my mind at ease perhaps I should take Gidget to the UW of Madison Veterinarian School. They had specialists who were trained in canine heart issues and could do a complete exam of Gidget's heart.

I said, "I think that sounds like a good plan. I'll call the university when I get home."

As I suspected, it was not inexpensive, but I felt five hundred dollars was a small price to pay for the peace of mind of knowing Gidget's heart really was healthy. This knowledge would also help me make a more educated and sound decision as to how to move forward.

I also reached out via email to Cheryl letting her know I was going to have Gidget's heart evaluated. I wanted to be upfront with her, and I was also hoping that perhaps she had other medical records for Gidget I wasn't aware of.

Cheryl emailed me back, saying she would contact Dr. Victor, the veterinarian who had made the diagnosis about Gidget's heart, and ask her to fax Gidget's medical records to me. When two weeks went by and I hadn't received anything, I emailed Cheryl again. This time she gave me the name of the clinic where Dr. Victor practiced. I called the clinic and spoke to the receptionist, who said she would relay the message. When another week passed with no call from Dr. Victor, I called again and left another message. The third time I called, I sensed frustration and irritation in the receptionist's tone.

"Haven't you called here before?" she asked.

I was somewhat taken aback by her reaction. "Yes, I have, but Dr. Victor hasn't called me back. I'd really appreciate it if I could talk to her."

Still sounding agitated, she said, "I'll see if she's available."

"Thank you."

A few moments later, Dr. Victor was on the phone. "How's Gidget doing?" she asked, her tone both excited and concerned. It caught me off guard.

"Well, as far as I know, she's fine," I replied. "But I'm concerned because I was told when I adopted her that she has a weak heart. I recently took her to my vet, and he feels her heart is fine. He said Gidget does have a heart murmur, but it's a common one found in dogs and nothing to be concerned with."

What I heard next stunned me into silence.

"Gidget is a very sick dog." Dr. Victor said. "She has Sick Sinus Syndrome (SSS) and needs a pacemaker."

When I finally found my voice again, I said, "I had no idea. This wasn't shared with me when I adopted Gidget. I was only told that she almost died when under anesthesia during a routine dental procedure."

Dr. Victor reiterated that Gidget was very sick. Still, in shock, I wasn't sure what else to say so I thanked her for her time and said goodbye.

It felt surreal. *How could this be,* I wondered? Gidget seemed fine to me. Was I missing something? So many questions ran through my mind, along with a growing feeling of anger. If she really was that sick, why had she been up for adoption and then put on a plane? And why wasn't I told how serious this was? Or the fact she needed a pacemaker? It didn't make any sense.

I went to my computer and googled "canine sick sinus syndrome." According to veterinarian and integrative pet care expert Dr. Karen Becker, "SSS is a condition in which the sinus node in the heart doesn't work as it should, resulting in long pauses between heartbeats. The sinus node doesn't consistently discharge an electrical impulse to trigger the heart to contract."

It's most often seen in older female dogs of certain breeds, including dachshunds. Some dogs with SSS have no symptoms, while symptomatic dogs typically have either a too-slow or a too-fast heartbeat. They can also show signs of weakness, fatigue, exercise intolerance, and fainting.

The treatment of choice for symptomatic dogs is a pacemaker. Medication can be used for some SSS canines, but they have an inconsistent track record, as well as side effects. The cost of surgery to implant a pacemaker—between $5,000 and $15,000!

My research left me even more perplexed, as I had not observed any of the signs of SSS in Gidget. I was now even more thankful I had set up an appointment at UW Madison Veterinary School, where they had the latest technologies to diagnose and treat health issues. In the meantime, I continued to pray that Gidget didn't have SSS.

A week later, Gidget and I made the two-hour trip to Madison. When we arrived, Dr. Henry, seasoned heart specialist and head of their cardiology department, said, "We will do a thorough examination and perform an electrocardiogram and echocardiogram. It will take about four hours, so if you want to do some shopping we will call you when we have the results."

Shopping was out of the question, as the cost to pay for this was going to set us back somewhat. But I remembered driving past a restaurant just a few minutes away, so I decided to hang out there and read a book I'd brought along and get a little something to eat.

Three hours later, I made my way back to the university to wait it out and was pleasantly surprised when after only ten minutes a vet technician came out to let me know the results were ready.

The first thing Dr. Henry said was, "Gidget's heart is perfectly healthy and normal."

I exhaled a sigh of relief! She then showed me the test results, explaining how this was determined through the two procedures they had performed.

I drove home that day giddy with happiness that Gidget was healthy, yet I still couldn't get Dr. Victor's incorrect diagnosis out of my mind. I knew I would share this information with Cheryl, not only because I was upset about the misinformation and the angst it caused me, but because I felt Cheryl should know Gidget wasn't sick.

When I arrived home, I emailed Cheryl with the good news and to tell her how relieved I was. Within a few hours I received her response, saying that she was relieved also. She then offered to take Gidget back and refund my adoption fee, plus reimburse me the $500 for the heart tests. She said she was still concerned I was going to spay Gidget and it could put her life in jeopardy.

This both perplexed and upset me. I had never even hinted that I might want to give Gidget back, quite the opposite: I loved her and considered her part of my family. Yes, I felt bad about going back on my word about not spaying her, but I was confident I had done everything I could to make sure she was healthy. I also knew in my heart that I was being called to stand in what I felt was the truth and to do what was best for Gidget.

About a week later, medical records, not from Dr. Victor, but from Dr. Frank, the vet who performed the dental cleaning and attempted spay, were faxed to my veterinarian's office. After Dr. Brenner read the report he told me that in his opinion Gidget was accidentally given too much anesthesia during the procedure, which likely caused her heart rate to drop as low as it did. It was a mistake that had nearly proven fatal for her.

While I still had some concern about putting Gidget under anesthesia, Dr. Benner provided me further peace of mind when he said he'd use an anesthesia they use for heart patients.

CHAPTER 8

Seizures

WITH GIDGET'S HEART problems behind us, I now looked forward to life getting back to normal.

Though Gidget still showed signs of anxiety at times, these moments seemed to grow fewer and farther between as she continued to settle into her new environment. For the next year things were wonderful—I was getting to know her more, snuggling with her every night on the sofa, taking her for rides in the basket on my bike, visiting the Farmer's Market where people loved to admire and pet her, and having her to keep me company in my writing cottage each day.

It also felt good to not have an agenda with Gidget as I did with Frankie and Joie. My time with Frankie was a life-changing experience and one I will always look upon fondly, but I didn't miss the fast pace it brought with it. I was genuinely enjoying a quieter and slower life.

It was early in November 2014 and nearing Gidget's first anniversary with us when I came across SoulCollage®, which as mentioned earlier was the intuitive process I would use to make the winter solstice card with Frankie's photo. This same card would become part of the sacred ritual I'd done when releasing her ashes in 2017. I was fascinated by the way working with images and collaging them, and then journaling, could open a channel of wisdom from within myself, much like working with oracle cards.

I wanted to become a SoulCollage facilitator, but I didn't know how I could leave Gidget for a two-and-a-half-day training. As had been the case with Frankie and Joie, I was never able to find a dog sitter to come to our home when we wanted to get away. Not many are comfortable expressing a dog's bladder and stimulating a bowel movement. But I really felt called to take the training and was determined to find a way to make it work.

When I talked to John about it, he understood the need I had to do this for myself. In the past he had tried to express our doxies' bladders, but he never did grow comfortable with it.

He said, "If you can find someone to check on Gidget during the day and express her, I'll do my best at night to do the same."

After doing some research and talking to friends, I found a gal in a nearby town who was a pet sitter. As it turned out, I already knew of her because she followed my work as a writer. She too had an interest in being a writer and had contacted me a few times in the past with questions about her writing endeavors.

I emailed her, asking if she'd consider taking care of Gidget for me while I was away at the training. She said she had never expressed an animals' bladder before, but she agreed to come over to talk with me about it.

Our visit went well, though she did have some apprehension after I demonstrated how to express Gidget's bladder. I felt she would be able to handle it, and though I was concerned for Gidget I knew I had to give this a chance and trust it would work out. Besides, I'd only be a little over two hours away. I could return home if there was a problem.

Finally the weekend arrived, and with a mix of excitement and apprehension I said goodbye to John, Kylie and Gidget and headed to the monastery where the training was to be held. When I got there I was filled with delight, as it was surrounded by woods with walking paths and large old wise trees. It was just what I needed.

It was unusually cold, yet each morning before the training began I found myself walking the winding paths of the woods around the quiet and neatly kept grounds. In the distance, I saw wetlands and heard the sounds of a variety of birds. I was alone during these walks, which despite the blustery weather surprised me. Though the wind stung my face, it made me feel vibrantly alive and I couldn't help but think the others were missing out.

Together with the training, these glorious moments in nature were like a soothing balm for my soul. Time flew as we meditated, collaged and journaled what the images represented for us, and before I knew it, it was Sunday afternoon and my name was being called to receive my certification. As I walked to the center of the room, I was overcome with tears. I felt empty but full all at the same time. It had been so long since I'd done something like this for myself. My heart was swimming in gratitude.

I remained in this state of serenity right up until I walked into the house and learned the pet sitter and John weren't able to express Gidget's bladder. This was distressing to say the least.

John told me that Gidget had had frequent accidents, which I was relieved to hear because at least some urine had come out. It also meant however that she wasn't able to completely empty her bladder, which was concerning because it could eventually lead to a bladder infection. As guilt set in, I hoped this wouldn't be the case. I also couldn't help but be disappointed that the likelihood of similar weekend outings was slim to none. I couldn't leave her again, not as long as I was the only one who could express her.

There were other issues as well, including her continued anxiety when I left the house. When John was home he tried his best to comfort her, often unsuccessfully; then I'd feel guilty not only for leaving her but because he had to listen to her cry.

Though John was wonderful about honoring my needs, I was acutely aware that if he had his wish, we would not be caring for another disabled dog. Unlike Frankie, whose IVDD had taken us by surprise, I had adopted Joie and Gidget with full knowledge of what an undertaking it was. Yes, each had wiggled her way into John's heart, but that didn't erase the fact that caring for them was not a choice he would have made.

Two months after I'd returned from my training I took Gidget for a routine wellness exam. When during the visit it was suggested I schedule a dental cleaning for her, I didn't object. I knew her heart was healthy and besides, Dr. Benner took the extra precaution with the type of anesthesia he used. I made the appointment for two weeks later and left the office feeling like we were on the right track with regard to Gidget's healthcare. Little did I know our journey was going to take a frightening turn.

The following Friday evening, I was lying on the couch reading a book. Gidget was nestled between my legs and we were warm and snug under a blanket.

I felt her moving, then realized it was more like a *thrashing*. I immediately sat up and threw the blanket off her. Her tiny body was convulsing in spasms. Initially, I thought she was having a bad dream, but her movements were erratic. I then noticed her eyes were rolled back in her head and foam was coming out the side of her mouth.

Though I had never seen anything like this before I knew in my gut what was happening. I called out to John, who was in the bedroom, "John! John! Gidget is having a seizure!"

He ran into the living room. "What do we do?"

"I don't really know," I said, surprised at how calm I sounded. Though I knew nothing about seizures my instinct told me to keep gently stroking Gidget's back, which I was doing as I softly repeated, "It's okay, sweetheart. You're going to be okay."

I was trying to convince myself as much as her, because inside I was scared she was going to die.

The tremors lasted for about two minutes and then stopped, leaving Gidget looking around the room, clearly disoriented. I scooped her into my arms and wrapped the blanket around her, reassuring her I was there and that everything was okay. I also noticed she had peed on the sofa, but that would have to wait while I comforted her.

She then began to whimper, and while she still seemed confused, I noticed her eyes were no longer rolled in the back of her head. It would be approximately another fifteen minutes before she looked like herself again. I sat her down on the floor and she was a bit shaky at first, but then made her way to her food bowls in the kitchen and lapped up water.

It was now past nine p.m., after my vet's office hours, and they didn't do emergency calls. I wasn't sure that Gidget needed immediate care, but I was concerned enough to call the number of the nearest emergency clinic.

When I told the woman who answered the phone what had just happened, she asked me a few questions, including whether it had ever happened before.

"Not that I'm aware of," I replied, "but I adopted Gidget from a rescue so I can't say for sure. It is the first time it's happened in my care."

She said they encouraged owners to bring their pets in, but I was hesitant. The clinic was forty-five minutes away and since Gidget seemed fine now I didn't want to put her through an unnecessary ordeal. I did, however, speak with a veterinarian technician at the clinic, and after this conversation I felt comfortable waiting—assuming she did not have another seizure—until the morning to see my local veterinarian. Needless to say, I barely slept that night, as I was too busy listening to Gidget's every move and sound she made. Thankfully, she seemed to be resting comfortably.

By six a.m. the next morning I was on the phone with the vet's office, once again explaining the events of the previous evening. The receptionist listened without interrupting me, then said she would have Dr. Benner call me when he got in around mid-morning.

The phone rang a few minutes past eleven. When I shared with him what I'd experienced the night before, Dr. Benner concurred with the veterinarian technician, and my own suspicion, that Gidget had likely had a seizure.

"What causes seizures?" I asked, still unable to believe this had happened to her. "The rescue I adopted her from didn't mention her having any seizures."

"We often don't know what causes them. Gidget could have had one since she's been living with you but you weren't there to witness to it. On the other hand, it could also have been her first."

While I realized that could have been the case, it still seemed unlikely as I was with her pretty much every day.

"What can be done for them?" I asked.

"We really don't do anything unless they begin to occur more frequently. This could be an isolated case and Gidget may never have another one."

"I hope so. It was hard to see her go through that."

"I understand, but keep in mind that dogs don't know when it's happening. This was harder on you than it was on her."

"This is good to know," I said, relieved that at least Gidget wasn't aware. Still, it was cause for concern and at Dr. Benner's suggestion I postponed her dental cleaning that had been scheduled for the following week.

As I thanked him and ended the call, I prayed this would turn out to be an isolated incident. But the next month, almost to the day of her first seizure, Gidget went into convulsions again, waking me out of a sound sleep at eleven p.m.

CHAPTER 9

Wheelchair Therapy

THE NEXT ELEVEN months were a roller coaster ride. But for a two-month reprieve, Gidget had a seizure every five weeks, each lasting two to three minutes. Most often her seizures occurred overnight, which made me wonder if perhaps she had had them before and I just slept through them.

I kept a journal tracking the day, time, and duration of each seizure and stayed in touch with Dr. Benner. I was becoming increasingly concerned, but he reminded me that typically nothing is done in terms of medication until seizures are occurring more than once a month.

He told me that once a drug is introduced to control seizures it is usually a lifetime commitment; there was also the possibility that the medication would stop working at some point. Then again, the seizures could eventually stop on their own. Given all this, he felt a conservative approach was best. We needed to give it more time.

While I appreciated and trusted Dr. Brenner completely, I was not satisfied with just sitting back and waiting. I am someone who needs to know the whys of things, which usually means conducting thorough research. I have found this to be both a blessing and a curse, as I can drive myself crazy. There are times when one just has to accept that some things are a mystery.

This was not one of those times. I wanted to know more about Gidget's seizures. I thought perhaps there was something I was or wasn't doing, something that could be changed to help her. Before I knew it I was trying to learn all I could about canine epilepsy. One of the most helpful sites I found was canine-epilepsy.com, a non-profit organization that provides information and support to those who love and care for an epileptic pet. It would turn out to be an invaluable resource, and one that brought me a great deal of comfort.

The site contained many articles about potential causes and theories. Most importantly, they offered advice and stories from others on how to live and care for a pet with seizures.

What I liked most, though, was that they embraced holistic treatment options as well as Western medicine. For many years I had believed in an integrative approach to healthcare for both pets and people, and after reading that holistic treatments have helped animals with seizures, I began searching for a veterinarian who specializes in Chinese medicine and acupuncture. This led me to Dr. Annie, whose office was about two hours from my home. I liked what I read about her, so despite the distance I scheduled an appointment to see if she could help Gidget.

Meeting with Dr. Annie was a rewarding experience, both educationally and because of the genuine compassion I felt from her. After she took Gidget's vitals and gave her an acupuncture treatment, Dr. Annie advised putting Gidget on a Chinese herb which had been effective in treating some animals with seizures. There was no guarantee, just like anything else, but I was comfortable with the advice and hopeful that it would help Gidget.

As the months wore on, though, Gidget continued to have seizures and at the same frequency—four to five weeks apart. I kept Dr. Annie informed via email and in the meantime continued to study the information on canine-epilepsy.com. After a while Dr. Annie added another Chinese herb to Gidget's regimen, and I continued to have hope that we could get Gidget's seizures under control without pharmaceuticals.

I also decided to contact Dawn, the animal communicator, for an appointment. Dawn had helped me with my other dogs over the years, and I completely trusted her intuitive guidance; I had also come to consider her a good friend. In my session with her, Dawn said that perhaps Gidget was picking up on my energy and was trying to help me shake something loose.

I do believe animals can pick up on their humans' energy, and that they are much more attuned to energy than most people. I wasn't quite sure what Gidget could be picking up from me, but I stayed open to the idea.

As the end of the year approached, Gidget's seizures increased, and in early December she had three within two weeks. After months of taking the herbs without success, I knew I had to seriously consider adding a medication.

After yet another overnight seizure, I called Dr. Brenner's office and was relieved when the receptionist said he was available to see Gidget in an hour. By this point, I was frazzled to the core and tried to brace myself for what was sure to be a difficult visit. Though he had been my primary vet for many years and had my utmost respect, we didn't always see eye-to-eye because of what I sensed was his mistrust of holistic treatment.

Sure enough, when I met with him that morning I was upset and intimidated by the way he questioned me about the efficacy of the herbs Gidget was taking. I had encouraged him over the past few months to reach out to Dr. Annie to learn more about the herbs, but for whatever reason, it didn't happen. This left me feeling frustrated.

I could hear the quiver in my voice as I said, "What I'd really like is to have both of you on Gidget's team. I'm not against Western medicine. But I feel like you're against holistic treatment. I would never do something to harm Gidget or put her life in danger."

What I was saying, in a roundabout way, was that I felt judged. I was trying not to cry, but the months of stress and frustration had taken their toll and the tears finally spilled out.

Dr. Benner placed his hand on mine. "I know you're doing what you feel is right for Gidget. I also wish I had more time to be educated about alternative treatment."

I was both surprised and relieved when he said this, as well as hopeful that perhaps we could move forward together to help Gidget. After talking about the various seizure medications and their costs, we decided to put Gidget on Potassium Bromide (KBr). It seemed much more benign than phenobarbital, which has many side effects and must be administered according to a strict schedule.

Gidget would need to take the KBr every day, but should I miss a dose for some reason, it wouldn't be detrimental. It also didn't have a lot of side effects, though one she would likely experience was ataxia—a loss of coordination or unbalanced gait due to sensory dysfunction. Dr. Brenner assured me that this would likely subside as her body became accustomed to the medication. She should be herself again within about two weeks.

This was very worrisome to me, as she was already compromised in her hind legs due to IVDD, but since nothing else was working it seemed our only hope of getting her seizures under control.

As predicted, the ataxia was visible within two days of beginning the medication. Gidget was having difficulty walking. At times it appeared as if she was drunk. It broke my heart to observe the lack of coordination in her hind legs, but I kept reminding myself that this was probably temporary.

Two weeks later, however, she was still not able to walk well; in fact, she often stumbled or pulled herself along on the floor. I didn't know how other dogs fared under the same circumstances, but clearly Gidget was not regaining her mobility as Dr. Brenner and I had hoped. That's when I remembered the wheelchair Frankie and Joie had used.

I had learned over the years that wheelchairs not only help paralyzed dogs move around but are also used as therapy to help them maintain their muscle tone and prevent atrophy until they regain their mobility. I was hoping it might do the same for Gidget so that when her body adjusted she'd be strong enough to support her backend.

Since it was winter and snowy, she wouldn't be able to exercise in the wheelchair outside. Fortunately, we have a thousand-square-foot finished basement, so twice a day, once in the morning and once in the late afternoon, Gidget began wheelchair therapy sessions.

Once she was strapped in the wheelchair, I'd have her follow me to the other side of the large open room with a treat in my hand as her reward. She was hesitant and a bit clumsy at first, but in no time at all she was flying back and forth across the room in the wheels.

In the evenings, I'd massage her hind legs and up and down and along the outside of her spine to encourage blood flow to the weak areas.

After approximately six weeks, between the wheelchair therapy and the massage, and her system finally adjusting to the medication, she was back to her little spunky self. What a relief and joy this brought John and me!

CHAPTER 10

Unraveling

PAINFUL SIDE EFFECT aside, the KBr was successful in stopping Gidget's seizures. As we settled back into normal life, I'd often think back on the conversation I'd had with my mom in December, a few days after I started Gidget on the medication.

As we do every year, we had gotten together for lunch at a local restaurant to celebrate the Christmas season. She listened compassionately as I told her how tired I felt. Gidget and I had been through so much more than I could have ever anticipated, and frankly, I was often overwhelmed.

I was feeling the stress of caring for special needs dogs for so long—nine years at that point. Other than a four-month break in between Frankie's passing and adopting Joie, then another before adopting Gidget, it had been non-stop and I was beginning to feel exhausted from it all. I was also the primary caretaker for Kylie, our English yellow Labrador. Kylie had been a laid back and low maintenance dog, but at ten years old she was beginning to slow down from arthritis and would need more care moving forward.

I also told my mom about my awkward conversation with Dr. Benner about the Chinese herbs. Though he had to smooth over the situation, I was still struggling with the feelings of being judged with regard to my decisions about Gidget's care.

"Perhaps," Mom said, "when Gidget is gone someday, you will need to take a break."

I broke down crying. "But who will take care of all the special needs dogs then?"

Anyone listening to me would have thought I had taken care of *every* special needs dog in the world, or at least those with IVDD. The reality was that Gidget was only the third special needs dog I'd brought into my life. But it *felt* like I had taken care of so many more. My mom wasn't the first person I had told of my exhaustion, either; in fact, I had been saying the same thing to John and close friends for several months.

What I wouldn't realize until two years later was the full weight of the responsibility I felt to take care of these dogs. If I didn't continue to do this, who would? What would happen to those dogs who needed help? I couldn't bear the thought. But in the moments I was alone and honest with myself, I began to picture a life when I was not taking care of a dachshund with IVDD.

It was a struggle to hear myself think in this way, and there were times when I was consumed by guilt. For all the inner work I had done at this point, and my continued commitment to living a self-examined life, I still had moments of worrying what others thought about me and my choices.

I had blogged often about the joy I felt caring for special needs dogs. It had been rewarding and at one point was a life purpose I embraced with open arms. I was proud of the positive impact I'd made by sharing my experiences with dogs with IVDD, and for a long time, I hoped this work would be my legacy. Yet I couldn't deny that something had changed; nor could I continue to bury the disconcerting feelings that were consuming me more and more each day.

Once again, I felt my identity was at stake. I had often thought about how we tend to put people in a box and don't allow them to move outside that box, even when they desperately want to. I know I'd certainly done this with people I admired. Even worse, we often confine ourselves to the box for fear of how others will react if we leave it.

Like many people, I sometimes felt envious if someone I admired was living in a way I wanted to live or experiencing something I wanted to experience. I often downplayed this feeling to make myself feel better, but what I didn't realize was that the envy was telling me something important. It was telling me that I really wanted to grow and expand but was allowing my insecurity to hold me back. This fear about moving forward was also connected to my feeling trapped by my responsibilities of caring for a dog with special needs.

For the longest time, when moments of questioning arose, I'd quickly push them away, though it was clear from my blog posts that I was expanding my writing to include such topics as mysticism, nature, transitional times in one's life, oracles, and spirituality.

A new space within me was opening. I had a growing interest and understanding of how the Universe is continually presenting us with opportunities to live from new perspectives; we must simply be willing to take the time to slow down and listen. Perhaps everything I was feeling of late was preparing me for a shift that was trying to move into my consciousness.

I recalled that during my sabbatical a few years earlier I had set the intention of wanting to understand more about the wisdom from *all* animals, not just the animals I'd shared my life and home with. I wanted to know more about those I'd encountered in the wild, such as deer, rabbits, birds, Sandhill Cranes, and opossum. I knew the profound lessons I'd learned from my dogs over the years were now driving my curiosity about potential messages from other animals.

During my sabbatical I meditated every day and worked with an oracle card deck, pulling a card each day. This helped me tap into my intuition on a deeper level. Journaling what I was feeling, thinking, and discovering enabled me to gain insight into my inner world. I began to see a clearer picture of what was calling to me at that time in my life.

I recalled one warm day a few years earlier when I cranked open a window of my writing cottage to find a family of frogs dead inside the windowsill. It broke my heart.

Though I knew it was an accident, that they must have gotten caught inside when I closed the window, I felt responsible. When I couldn't shake the feelings, or the image in my mind, I contacted Dawn.

She agreed that it could have been an accident, but she also encouraged me to explore the possibility that there was something about the frogs' deaths that pointed to an end or a letting go of something in my own life. Though

I didn't fully understand it at the time, I didn't ask more questions; nor did I pursue it further to see if there might have been some helpful insight to glean from the incident.

As I moved through my sabbatical, my need to explore and understand more how the Universe guides us kept growing. For as long as I could remember, I had never believed in coincidences, but rather that everything happens for a reason, even when we may not understand it in the moment.

Though I grappled with my understanding of God, I've always believed there is something bigger than us in the invisible realm, guiding and supporting us. This guidance often comes in the form of signs and symbols, be they animals, an oracle card, meditation, or new ways of creativity. All are a part of a language that can help us to connect to our intuition.

All of this is ancient knowledge has been around for thousands of years. We have access to it if we choose. The challenge is that as a society we've moved away from this wisdom because of our endless striving for material possessions and our belief that they will bring us happiness.

Over the past several years this was something I had been consistently working on—shedding the layers of old beliefs to uncover what was essential for me, even if it was not necessarily what society dictated.

The more layers I peeled away, the more I wondered whether this was part of Gidget's teaching and why she had come into my life. Was she an animal oracle, guiding me to the next phase of my journey?

CHAPTER 11

White Wolf Laiola

JUST A FEW short months after Gidget came to live with us, I began to call her my Buddha dog.

It was true that she loved to cuddle, but she also had this confident air about her. I sensed also that she was very wise.

Eleven months after we adopted Gidget, I went through a period of profound grief over the loss of a friendship. In many ways, it felt to me like Nikki had died, and, oddly, I think my heart could have handled that more easily.

John had also become very fond of Nikki; he took her under his wing and invested much of his time to help her, both personally and professionally. It was a labor of love that we both felt called to do.

When Nikki made the decision to get a divorce, John and I stood by her; we even opened up the lower level of our home for her to live while she envisioned her dream life and got back on her feet. John lovingly added a small kitchen to the space, which included a large living area and bedroom. We wanted her to feel at home as she moved through a pivotal and transitional time.

It wasn't long before the three of us were sharing meals together and hanging out on the weekends on the deck and sitting in front of the chiminea. We bonded over our many conversations about the ups and downs of life and began to feel much like a family. As John and I never had children of our own, it was rewarding and fulfilling to be there for Nikki, much like parents are for their children. John and I grew to love and care about her and would have done anything to protect her from harm.

The trouble began when I could no longer handle what John and I both felt was a destructive path Nikki was taking regarding a young man in her life. I loved her so much and tried to help her see that the relationship she was in was on many accounts unhealthy. This caused both John and me a great deal of angst, which eventually caused the demise of our relationship with Nikki. Though it had been some time in coming, when the end came, it came abruptly.

It wasn't an easy time for John or me. During especially difficult moments, I held onto the "everything happens for a reason" credo I've always believed in. There had to be a purpose in this for each of us, and together, as a couple. I didn't want to be bitter or hold a grudge, though I was struggling with both.

As John worked through his grief, he seemed to become a different man. His heart was battered because of the time and love he had invested in Nikki, not only in her personal life, but by helping build the studio of her dreams. But this experience had also opened him in a way that I had not witnessed before. Learning to care for, and be there, for someone who needed his guidance as Nikki did had made him more compassionate. It had cracked his heart wide open.

I decided to seek counseling to help me understand what it was I needed to learn from the experience. A part of me wanted the friendship back more than anything; however, another part of me recognized that I'd been sensing for quite some time that something was "off," though I couldn't define it.

There were times during the friendship that I felt held back from moving forward with my own aspirations. I was giving so much of my energy to Nikki that there seemed to be little left for me. What's more, her needs only increased over time, which meant that I was feeling more and more exhausted.

The counseling I went through with Pam, who was also a life coach, helped me to find my way back to myself. During one of our sessions she introduced me to the idea that I could talk to Nikki without a face-to-face connection.

She encouraged me to set aside some time and tell Nikki how hurt I was, how I felt betrayed, and to forgive her. On an energetic level, Pam said, Nikki would know, and it would help to release the toxic chord between us.

I was skeptical at first, but a few days later, while sitting in my writing cottage, a place where I'd spent so much time with Nikki, I felt it was time to make this connection. I'd eventually come to understand what this time in my life had to teach me. It felt good saying my peace, forgiving, and cutting the ties, but it would take time for the pain to fall away.

During my last counseling session with Pam, I was pleasantly surprised when she suggested taking me through a guided visualization. As I lay on the sofa of her home office, I was a little nervous. I had never experienced a guided visualization before and had no idea what to expect, but I also felt comfortable with Pam and trusted her.

Pam waited for me to get settled, then turned on calming music and gently began guiding me through the visualization. In it, I found myself coming to the base of a mountain. A stream gurgled nearby, and there was a large boulder before me that I felt called to sit on. I saw myself wrapped in a white hooded scarf my mom had recently knit for me.

A moment later, I saw in the distance a white wolf. At first I felt fear, but soon enough I sensed she was there to help me. I sat there, staring at the exquisite beauty of this wolf as she crept closer and eventually lay down at my feet. I remember how I was overcome with a feeling of deep and true love.

As we sat together at the base of the mountain, I felt safe and protected, and as if nothing could hurt me again. It was then that I saw a large heart with flames shooting out from all sides. I heard a message from the wolf that even though my heart had been deeply hurt I was not to let it close. It was essential to keep my heart open. She reminded me of my empathetic and compassionate nature. To shut my heart down would not only be a disservice to not only myself but to those I loved. There would be new friends I'd meet along my journey.

As I drove home down the country roads after the session, I knew I had to find a way to capture what I'd just experienced. It occurred to me that I was scheduled to take the training as a SoulCollage facilitator in one month's time, and suddenly I knew what I would do to keep this experience alive.

When I arrived home, I searched online for different images of white wolves until I found the one that spoke to me as the one I saw during the visualization. I also printed out a picture of a mountain Dawn, who lives in Alaska, had recently posted on her Facebook page. It was that mountain I had seen during the visualization. When John came home later that day, I asked him to take a photo of me in the hooded knit scarf.

I gathered all the images and then collaged them onto a 5 x 8 piece of cardstock, which is commonly used in the SoulCollage process. Once it was complete, I placed it on the altar in my writing cottage. It was a reminder of what I had experienced and to continue to stay tuned in to what my heart felt.

Even though I'd have moments of wondering if what I experienced was "real," there was no doubt that it had changed me. Somehow I felt comforted and didn't feel alone. I had found in this white wolf an ally to guide and support me.

I didn't think much about the white wolf after that, at least not on a conscious level. Then, one night two years after her initial visit, she popped into my mind as I was I drifting off to sleep. I decided to test if there was indeed something more to our connection than what I'd experienced during the guided visualization.

I silently said, *What's your name, white wolf?*

I didn't really expect a response, though I figured if I did get one it would be a common name. I was quite surprised when I heard *Laiola,* which I had never heard before and was quite unusual. I was still a little skeptical, but it felt right in my heart. I decided I'd google it in the morning to see if I found anything. I was smiling as I drifted off to sleep.

The next morning, I took to the internet to see if there was such a name as Laiola and, if so, whether there was any symbolism connected with it. When I wasn't able to find anything, I took it as confirmation that what I'd heard the night before was meant solely for me.

Some may think there isn't anything to this; some might think it's crazy, but that doesn't matter. I had this *knowing* in my heart. There was also, however, a part of me that still worried about judgment from others, so it would be some time before I felt comfortable sharing this experience.

CHAPTER 12

Feared Creature

IT WAS REFRESHING to know I had a special connection with a white wolf named Laiola. There was also little doubt in my mind that I had drawn the experience to me, having set the intention to be open to wisdom from more of the animal kingdom. What I had not considered, however, was that I might attract experiences not only from animals I considered cute, cuddly or majestic, but those commonly thought of as ugly, repulsive, and even scary. The following summer I would have an encounter with such an animal, one I now consider to have helped me make a pivotal shift in my perspective, and heal a past emotional wound.

According to *Animal Speak* by Ted Williams, this creature is one of rebirth, resurrection, initiation, and wisdom. He also shares that of all the animals, this is one of considerable controversy and paradox.

One evening in early August 2015, Kylie, Gidget and I were headed to a small wooded area near my home when I noticed, about two feet off the end of the driveway, the most brilliant emerald green snake. I was unsure if she was alive, so I walked with trepidation up to her only to realize she was dead. It was then I noticed two baby snakes next to her, and two more a few feet away. All had perished.

Holding Kylie and Gidget's leashes taut to keep them back, I just stood there, overcome with sadness as I looked at the snakes. Suddenly an awful thought occurred to me—had I accidentally run them over? I didn't remember hitting them, but there was no way to know for sure.

As I walked into the woods with Kylie and Gidget, I couldn't shake the image of the snake family from my mind. When the next day I still couldn't let go of it, I sent an email to Dawn telling her of my encounter and how upset I was.

I didn't have to wait long for her reply. "Snake medicine can mean big changes," she wrote. "The fact that you saw the snakes in this way and opened yourself to deeper emotions may indicate that Snake is somehow initiating you."

After reading her email I wasn't sure if there was a teaching here for me. Part of my hesitation, I realized, had to do with the fact that it involved snakes, and dead ones at that. What could that possibly mean? And what did Dawn mean when she said Snake might be "initiating" me? I wasn't quite able to wrap my mind around it.

Dawn then reminded me of a shed snakeskin I'd found a few months earlier among some dried leaves in the garden. I was fascinated by it, so much so that I had mentioned it to Dawn. I had bent down to examine it closer, but when I tried to pull it from the leaves it tore in two.

"Finding the discarded skin of a snake may be a hint to release a limited perspective that we have outgrown or to shed old ways," she said.

Dawn explained that encountering the family of snakes dead in the road may mean something else altogether. It was unusual, she said, for a mother snake to be with her babies, as most species of snake don't take care of their young. She prompted me to consider the possibility that there was a mother/child connection here.

She also suggested I think about the fact that the snakes had died while trying to cross the road. Was there a message here about me being immobilized in my own life?

Dawn encouraged me to sit with these clues for a while and see what came to me.

"Snake often challenges us to work for our wisdom," she said.

Dawn had certainly given me a lot to think about. *Was there something here that could positively guide me?* There was much going on in my psyche at the time, so perhaps there just may be something I could learn from Snake.

The following day I wrote back to her. "I'm still pondering Snake. Shedding old ways of seeing and letting go of the 'old' body with the snake shed I saw resonates with me."

I wanted to understand more. I wanted to learn how to dance with the wisdom of Snake. I asked Dawn if she was up for playing with this and to see where it might lead. She was happy to accommodate my request! We set up a time to talk via video connection.

As we began the conversation, I told Dawn how I'd been asking myself over and over, *What does this all mean?*

In one way I felt the encounter related to my mother.

"I've had to be strong for my mom the last year, as she has gone through a great loss. Seeing the baby snakes separated from their mother, I can relate to my close relationship with my mom. She has always been strong for me. But I've felt this shift and that it is now my time to be strong for her. While I know this is the natural flow of life, it isn't always easy."

As I gave voice to my thoughts, I also realized this was about my relationship with the dogs in my life, specifically the two children's books and two memoirs I had written about them, as this was a way in which many people had come to identify me.

"I struggle at times because I feel myself growing in a new and expanded direction. But I'm afraid to do so because my public identity is so tied to dogs. Letting go of that connection isn't something I wish to do completely. But I also find myself wanting to broaden and open to the wisdom of *all* animals. So yes, I guess you could say my 'skin' is getting bigger."

On another level, I could see a correlation with the way my body was changing as I moved through my menopausal years. There were times I was uncomfortable with how I was changing physically and I was trying to find peace with it, no easy task in our youth-obsessed culture. At one time I could look at myself naked in the mirror and be okay with what I saw, but these days that wasn't always the case.

The more Dawn and I talked the more I realized I did need to look at what was stopping me from being true to myself; for example, the lingering concern about others' opinions of me. Though this had lessened over the years due to the deep inner work I had done, I could not deny that others' criticism, real or imagined, sometimes caused me to second guess the direction I was feeling called to take.

Dawn reminded me that not everyone is ready or open for teachings from Snake. It can be difficult, but the rewards are worth it. Animals are trying to help us see the truth of *what is*.

My willingness to do this dance with Snake and the discussion I was having with Dawn was opening new channels from within; they were also confirming certain feelings I was having, though I found it difficult to express them.

Dawn said, "What we are doing here—in this dance—is helping give voice to the event and the encounter that speaks to your psyche. Signs are all around us, and the world continually speaks to us. It asks powerful questions such as, 'What does the snake in the road say to you?'"

Chuckling, I agreed. "Though those questions can sound crazy. Thinking outside the box, such as talking about the teachings we can glean from a dead snake, isn't something often encouraged in our culture, and it can feel scary. The fear of judgment should we express this out loud is real. That's why it's so important to find someone with whom we feel comfortable and safe so we can look at things we are sometimes afraid to look at alone."

Dawn nodded. "It helps," she said, "to open to the feelings, possibilities, and thoughts we might not have otherwise considered. Furthermore, expressing our perceptions helps to clear something within. By being heard—and by hearing ourselves—we gain insight into things we didn't think we knew. And by sharing our thoughts like this, we are both tapping into a larger flow."

I began to understand that this encounter with Snake was about looking beyond what I was seeing as well as what perhaps I *wasn't* seeing. More importantly, it was about addressing the feelings I was afraid to feel that were occurring at this time in my life.

I was curious as to how I could relive the experience of seeing the dead mama snake and her babies in a dream.

"How do I do that?" I asked her.

"In many ways, it *is* a dream," she said. "so you might begin by retelling your encounter as if it happened in a dream."

She pointed out the fact that the snakes died in front of my driveway, not anyone else's. She also prompted me to think about what a driveway is suggesting, as a path that leads away from my home, which is my personal space, to the outside world. She talked about seeing my car as the vehicle for my personal traveling self.

"In dream language," she explained, "a car parked in a driveway might suggest an obstacle between your home and the outer world. As you venture out of your home, you are stopped in your path by the dead snake and her babies. Now, what does that image say to you?"

I could feel my mind expanding even though I couldn't necessarily define it. It was interesting that for most of my life I couldn't even look at a snake. Now here I was exploring what seeing one could possibly mean.

Suddenly, I found myself curious about snakes. Dawn lived with two snakes and often shared photos of them on her Facebook page. Before, I had never been interested in looking at them, but now I did, and I was fascinated. I was eager to learn whatever wisdom Snake was trying to share with me.

"So often we are influenced by what we see in the media," I told Dawn during one of our conversations, "and then we get stuck in our beliefs and also judgments. But in seeing those judgments, and through my willingness to look at Snake, I've opened myself to a gift!"

A wave of emotion overcame me as I once again recalled the mama snake. "She was such a pretty snake, and the most exquisite shade of emerald green."

In fact, her color reminded me of a shade of green I'd seen a few months earlier and how the color had spoken to me. It felt like I'd never seen that color in that way before. Now here it was again in this snake I encountered. I wanted to cry. My heart was cracked open because of the beauty I saw in that snake even though she had died.

After the initial dance with Snake and her medicine, I recalled how a silence fell between Dawn and me—a depth of feeling that transcended language.

After we said goodbye to each other, I sat for a few more moments in reflection. I realized that Snake was sharing wisdom that I didn't need to prove anything to anyone. All that mattered was that this experience was *real* to me. Of course, if at some point I chose to share it I certainly could. Maybe it could also help someone else open something within and guide them on their path.

CHAPTER 13

Snake Ally

IT IS AMAZING to me how so many of us only believe what we see with our eyes. Even people who are more open spiritually can easily get caught up in the illusion our physical world presents, when really it is the invisible realm—signs, and symbols from nature and the Universe, our dreams, animals, and the mystical—from which we can gain more clarity for our lives.

Snake had provided me a remarkable teaching and I thought that was the end of it. That is, until Dawn and I talked again. She told me she had shared part of my snake story with her friend Tayria, who is a depth psychologist and dream therapist—and that Tayria had provided feedback for me. Immediately I was intrigued, as Dawn had mentioned Tayria to me before and I knew a bit about her work.

Indeed, the conversation in which Dawn conveyed Tayria's assessment was certainly an eye-opening one. Tayria explained that according to the Jungian school of thought, which is based on the work of Swiss psychiatrist and psychoanalyst Carl Jung, psychoanalysis is "designed to bring together the conscious and unconscious parts of the mind to help a person feel balanced and whole." A Jungian dream analyst, therefore, looks for what the dreamer *doesn't* share. Often the part that is ignored is the most profound, and because it is, we hold back and dance around it.

Tayria wanted to know if perhaps I felt like I had run over the snakes, and when Dawn told her I had wondered this myself but found the thought too hard to bear, she suggested I consider what I may inadvertently be crushing beneath the tires, as a metaphor of what I may be keeping hidden within my own psyche. She felt this was important, regardless whether I had actually run over the snakes or not. How would I feel if I knew I had in fact caused their deaths? Was there something I was pushing down?

Tayria also felt perhaps I could go deeper, which perplexed me. I didn't know what more there could possibly be for me to uncover with regard to the snakes. That said, after Dawn and I said goodbye once again I couldn't get the thought out of my head. I also suddenly started getting stomach pains and decided to lie down.

As I closed my eyes, hoping the ache in my stomach would soon pass, a vision flashed across my mind. It was a familiar vision, one I first had when I was twenty-nine and had continued to appear on and off for the last twenty-plus years. Each time it did, I'd quickly dismiss it. It was just too painful to look at. However, its defining feature, that of someone's hand, and someone touching me inappropriately, was ingrained in my memory.

There were many times when I'd questioned whether the vision was even real. Now, though, I wondered if perhaps it was connected to the message I had received from Snake. As quickly as that thought surfaced, I immediately pushed it to a far corner of my mind, where it would remain for the next few weeks.

Imagine my surprise when during my next video chat with Dawn I suddenly found myself sharing the disturbing vision I'd carried with me for over half my life. It had never been my intention to share this with anyone; I certainly hadn't planned to say anything to Dawn that day.

But now it was as if I had no control over the words coming out of my mouth, and before I realized it I had described a personal wounding from my childhood, an experience that until that moment I had not even given myself permission to validate, let alone discuss with another. It is important for me to share here that though I have chosen to keep specific details private, it had nothing whatsoever to do with my parents or siblings.

Now I had given voice, not only to the vision itself, but to the angst created by my questioning of my own mind all those years. Though I was stunned and crying, I also felt something quite remarkable; I felt like I'd come home to my body. Just writing this today, almost three years later, I can still feel the power of that moment, and the definite and marked shift that occurred within me. I remember feeling as if I was suspended in time, that I was able to feel whole in a way I'd never felt before, and I will always be grateful to Dawn for holding that sacred space for me in which to feel safe.

The next morning, after moving through my yoga practice, I sat down to meditate. I didn't meditate every day, but after reading of the many benefits I did try to do it a few times a week. I soon realized that when I meditated, even if only for five minutes, I felt much more grounded and my day flowed with more ease.

Most days, as soon as I closed my eyes it felt as if a thousand butterflies descended upon my stomach, fluttering wildly. But that day, as I lay on my yoga mat and focused on my breath, something felt different. I felt a new, deep sense of peace.

I was settling into this pleasant feeling when a few moments later I saw in my mind's eye an emerald green light enter my right foot and travel up the right side of my body. Halfway up, it shifted from a beam of green light to a snake! She continued along my right side and exited out the right side of my head, then reentered the left side, traveling down the left side of my body, exiting the bottom of my left foot.

I thought she might squiggle away at that point. But she then turned and began to move up between my legs, over my pelvic area and my belly before coming to rest between my breasts. We were now looking at each other. Her face was soft and sweet, and she had the kindest eyes. I didn't feel scared. I was comforted by her presence. I also sensed she was conveying to me that everything was going to be okay.

I took away from the experience that Snake, all those months ago, had been calling me to go deeper and let go of an excruciating vision that had haunted me for over two decades. She had been gently urging me to do the work to set myself free.

Again, some may think this is strange or weird, but what I felt in that moment was incredibly powerful. To deny it would feel like taking away what was another pivotal step in my healing.

Shortly after my mediation with Snake, I was reading a blog post by Maria Wulf, an artist whose work I followed, about fabric intuition dolls she was making. One of the dolls in particular caught my eye. It had a goddess-type woman stitched on it with green eyes and ornate symbols, but what really spoke to me was the green snake Wulf had stitched around the left arm. I knew I just had to have her!

That doll, which now holds a place of honor on the wicker chair in my writing cottage, is a beautiful reminder that what we sense, see and feel—be it in visions, dreams, or our inner world—is real. It's that intuitive part of us, whispering guidance and helping us to live from the truth of who we are.

My Snake story didn't end there. A few years later, the story of my encounter with the perished mama snake and her babies was included in the book, *The Ancient Wisdom of Snake*, written by none other than Dawn Brunke! As she was reviewing my story before sending off to her publisher, she had another observation about the meditation when I saw a snake enter my body.

In the Hindu tradition, she said, this is viewed as a Kundalini awakening. While I'd heard the term kundalini before and associated it with yoga, I didn't quite understand the broader scope of what it meant. When I did my inevitable internet search, I found this:

"Kundalini energy rests like a coiled serpent at the base of the spine. When this dormant energy flows freely upward through the seven chakras (energy centers) and leads to an expanded state of consciousness, it's known as a kundalini awakening."

This interpretation made perfect sense to me, and I was encouraged that Snake was continuing to weave in and out of my life as a helpful ally.

CHAPTER 14

Ollie the Horse

AS TIME PASSED, I had grown increasingly fascinated with the notion that we are being guided by Spirit *all the time,* and in so many more ways than meets the eye. I'd certainly witnessed this in various ways through nature and animals, including Gidget, who was by my side most days as my faithful companion and teacher. I had also seen it in the workshops I facilitated, whether it was SoulCollage or ancient wisdom gatherings I co-hosted with a friend.

Thanks to the messages I had received from Snake and the assistance of Dawn and Tayria, I felt satisfied that I was healed from the wounding I had experienced as a child. Seven months, later, however, I would discover there was still more inner work I needed to do.

Pam and I were in the planning stages of a workshop when she told me she sensed a conflict within me (though I hadn't expressed it in words) and offered me the gift of a one-on-one intensive with her and her horses.

"Along with deep breath work and meditation," she said, "working with the horses can help open those channels and release whatever is blocking you from moving forward."

A part of me was hesitant. Sure, I had turned to life coaching over the years when I needed an extra nudge to keep me moving forward, but I didn't quite understand how Pam's horses could help me. I also didn't want to share the details of my internal struggle. On the other hand, I was grateful for the offer and, I had to admit, more than a little curious.

One cool and sunny day in early May, I slowly drove down the long gravel driveway of Pam's quiet and serene ten-acre property. My whole body relaxed as I took in the view of the fences and trees that lined either side of the driveway. Eventually I came upon her horses grazing in the pasture, then Pam, who was waiting for me on her front porch.

We chatted briefly about the lovely weather, then Pam began explaining the process. She told me that the horse that would be guiding me had "chosen" to work with me three days earlier.

I was curious as to why it was three days, but I didn't ask as we began walking down the winding, grassy path that led to the area near the back of the property, where I knew Pam kept a tepee. In fact I had been inside the tepee once before, when I attended Pam's fall solstice gathering the previous year.

Sure enough, the tepee soon came into view. I followed Pam up a short set of stairs leading to the platform where the tepee sat, then waited as she untied the front flap and motioned for me to enter.

"We are going to start with having you set an intention," Pam said after we had settled into wooden Adirondack chairs. "After that, we will begin to work through what it is that may be blocking you."

Setting intentions wasn't new to me. I'd been doing this at various points on the spiritual and personal growth path I'd set out on in late 2004.

We sat for a few moments in silence as I contemplated and then set my intention. Pam then opened a bag she had sitting on her lap and pulled out an oracle deck called, *Touched by a Horse*.

Though I had worked with other oracle cards for years, I was not familiar with this particular deck. Also, I usually pulled cards at random, but Pam handed me the deck and said, "I want you to go through the deck one-by-one and pick two cards that you feel drawn to."

I took the deck from her and went to sit on the floor, crossing one leg over the other. I then began flipping each card over and placing it in front of me. Each one was more beautiful than the one before. I didn't think it would be possible for me to pick just two.

After I went through the entire deck I sat and stared at all the horse cards before me. It was then that two jumped out at me.

I picked them up and said, "These two are it." I paused to make sure. "Yes, these are definitely the two."

"Great. Now turn each one over and read the message on the back."

As I often do when working with oracle cards at home, I felt called to read them out loud. It seems when I do so, the message is able to sink in deeper. It also helps me understand how the information pertains to my particular situation.

The first card I chose to read was that of a young foal. There was something about her innocence that made my eyes fill with tears and tugged at my heart. During my life I had struggled with feeling a loss of innocence, but I was trying to find a way to see it as a gift that had helped to shape me into who I am.

The foal card spoke to certain areas of my life that I wanted to be innocent or naive about, and I knew I was being called to examine those areas now. The message was to delve deeper into what that innocence may bring me at this time in my journey. It was also about seeing innocence as a gift to my soul and a gift to others I interact with. It called for me to walk in that state of purity and to trust that vulnerability allows new experiences to come into my life.

I picked up the second card, that of a white stallion who appeared to me to be robust, regal, and confident. He was slightly on his haunches as if ready to gallop off at any moment and his tail was flying out behind him. The card's message was about celebration and release. It spoke to my desire to feel the same way, though a part of me was scared to do so.

I also saw this horse as helping me to celebrate the victories in my life, particularly those that felt small and insignificant, for each little moment was a step in the journey back to me. The card stated that acknowledging these achievements would assist in bringing about more of what I truly wanted.

I was reminded again of how it's our job to pay attention and look for the clues the Universe provides, then simmer in their meaning, listen for the answers, and eventually integrate them into our being.

Since my early forties, I had gradually begun owning the many parts of me while learning to stand more solidly in my truth. It hasn't always been easy. But there were these sparks provided to me along the way that I couldn't look away from. Many called to me to travel this path of the seeker in the hopes that I would continue to encounter new moments of light. And now I was about to experience yet another level of understanding with the help of one of Pam's horses.

After I read the cards, Pam and I left the tepee and began walking toward the pasture. As the figures of her horses—Dan, Quill and Ollie—came into view I took a deep breath. In the past I had been scared to be around horses because of their size, and though over the years my fear had quieted somewhat, I remained cautious.

Pam walked up to the gate and opened it, then we walked through and stood silently observing the horses who were grazing ten feet away.

After a few moments Pam said quietly, "Just stand still, right here in this spot. Don't move about. One of the horses will choose you. You'll know which one when he starts to make his way over to you."

A thrill of excitement ran through my body! *Who would choose me?* I wondered. True confession time: I was really hoping it would be Ollie. He had been part of the closing ceremony at the solstice the previous year, and I had been moved by his patience not only with me but the other participants as well.

During the ceremony, which had taken place in the barn, each person was invited to choose a feather from a basket that was passed around the circle. Pam instructed us to think of something we wished to let go of as we chose our feather. After we each had our feather, Pam began to make eye contact with each participant. That was our invitation to walk up to Ollie and place our feather in his mane. In the days to come, the feathers would eventually fall out in their own time; it was our job to trust that whatever we intended to let go of would eventually fall away as well.

When it was my turn, I approached Ollie and gently patted him on the nose before turning toward his mane. Holding my feather in one hand, I secured it with a rubber band Pam had handed me. I recall the wave of emotions I felt not only for myself but from the others gathered in the circle. The energy was so beautiful and palpable.

Now, as I stood there waiting to be chosen, I tried, despite my previous connection with Ollie, to be open to the other horses as well. I told myself that whatever happened was meant to be.

About five minutes had passed when Ollie started to inch his way toward me. I could barely contain my excitement but remained still. Before

I knew it, he stood before me in all his magnificent beauty and strength. I didn't know whether to jump for joy or cry, so honored was I that Ollie had chosen to be my guide!

Pam said, "We are now going to walk to the round pen. Ollie will follow."

Without saying anything to Ollie, we both turned toward the round pen and began to walk. Ollie did the same. When we got to the gate, Pam opened it as I stepped aside to allow Ollie to stroll through.

Pam instructed me to stay outside the pen as she joined Ollie inside the enclosure and closed the gate. He was now in the center of the pen with Pam standing beside him. Without speaking, Pam extended her left arm out to her side. As she did that, Ollie began to walk in a circle around the pen. Pam walked quickly toward him and was soon walking beside him.

Within a few moments, with no talking or visual instruction, he then began to trot when Pam picked up her pace. As Pam weaved back and forth, so did Ollie. They were dancing in the most beautiful and graceful way side-by-side. I was mesmerized by their connection. Again, I wanted to weep for it was breathtaking to witness.

It was then my turn to be with Ollie. As Pam opened the gate and stepped out, she invited me to step into the pen. At this point, Ollie was standing near the fence.

"Walk to the center of the pen," she said.

I did as she instructed.

"Now you are going to connect with Ollie without talking. You will be working with the energy of a horse. It's a way of communicating with them and guiding them to what you wish them to do."

I nodded and took a deep breath to ground myself, then turned to look into Ollie's big, soft brown eyes.

While I immensely enjoyed looking into the eyes of this gorgeous horse, I felt awkward and unsure of how to truly connect to him as I'd just observed Pam do.

Feeling a bit silly, I lifted my left arm out the side as Pam had done, hoping that Ollie would once again begin to walk in a circle.

He didn't move. I did it again. He then turned and looked the other way, leaving me to stare at his large backend. I wanted so badly to connect with him. I tried to will him with my mind to move, but nothing happened.

No matter what I did Ollie wouldn't budge, which was frustrating. Now that I was here and Ollie had chosen me, I wanted more than ever to connect with an animal in the way Pam had so beautifully demonstrated.

"To direct your energy means to build a connection with Ollie," Pam said as if reading my thoughts. "To do this, you must first find your center of power, your energy source, that center of gravity and feel the ground beneath your feet. This helps you to relax while also helping to build your physical vibration which then can be felt by the horse. You can then focus on the horse, feeling into his energy in motion, and this is what creates a mutual exchange between the two of you."

I nodded, realizing this wasn't something I could mentally "get" but would rather have to *feel* my way through.

"It's an ancient form of communication with human and horse, with both expressing themselves freely through a beautiful dance. It's feeling the flow of energy exchange that is being shared and released through each step and both fully enjoying each other's company."

I took in what Pam said as I tried again and again. But Ollie stood in place as if I wasn't even there.

Finally, Pam asked, "Do you know what the Native American call horses?"

"No, what?"

"Big Ol' dogs."

It was if a light bulb had gone off. I *knew* how to connect with dogs. After what had felt like hours with no response from Ollie, something suddenly shifted. I put one foot in front of the other and began to walk around the pen. A moment later, out of the corner of my eye I saw Ollie turn his head and start walking toward me. Before I knew it, he was beside me. Though I continued to walk slowly, inside I was jumping up and down with glee!

After a moment or two, Pam said, "Now pick up your pace to a slow trot."

When I sped up, so did Ollie. When I slowed down, Ollie followed that rhythm too. If I got too close to the front of his head, he would stop taking my lead.

Pam called out, "Be sure to stay behind Ollie's head and imagine you are in a bubble with him."

I did as she suggested and noted that Ollie and I were perfectly in sync, moving as one. Oh, how my spirit soared! I was dancing with Ollie!

This noble and powerful animal was only a few inches from me. It was so profound and moved me to tears.

As I tired and slowed down, so did Ollie. Coming to a halt, I stood next to him, breathing in the exquisite connection I just experienced. It felt as though I had entered a different realm.

"Great job, Barb!" Pam said as she joined us in the pen. "Next, I'm going to take you through a series of questions. This will help you to reflect on the intention you set earlier this morning."

I nodded in understanding.

"If you are comfortable you can place your hand on Ollie and keep it there while I ask you the questions. You don't have to answer them out loud, but if it helps you to do so that's fine too."

I didn't hesitate to place my hand on Ollie's side.

"Now I'd like you to close your eyes. Again, only if this feels comfortable for you."

I closed my eyes as Pam asked me each question. Some I answered out loud, some I contemplated in silence.

The purpose of the exercise was to guide me to focus inwardly on my intention and understand more deeply what was stopping me from taking the next steps in my life.

Suddenly, that old vision of being touched inappropriately as a child once against flashed through my mind, bringing with it a wave of emotions. How could this be, when I had done so much work to heal it? A part of me was so tired of it taking up space in my mind, but the other part wasn't sure how to move through it.

With my hand resting on Ollie's soft and muscular body, I felt an opening in my heart of hope and courage. This beautiful creature, the epitome of strength and grace, was something I wanted to become too.

When the last question had been asked and answered, Pam invited me to open my eyes when I was ready. She then walked Ollie to the gate of the pen. Before opening the gate, she asked me to disconnect from Ollie in whatever way felt comfortable for me.

"I like for the horse to make their own choice when parting ways and not force anything upon them. This is out of respect for the horse and acknowledging the gifts and their presence they shared with us."

Tears filled my eyes. It touched my heart to part in a mutually respectful way.

Placing a hand on Ollie's muzzle, I looked into his eyes and thanked him for having patience with me and for allowing me to spend time with him.

Pam opened the gate, and within a few moments Ollie sauntered out into the pasture. As we watched him, I asked Pam if I could have a picture with Ollie. I felt such gratitude for his willingness to play a role in guiding me to a more peaceful place.

"Of course."

Once Ollie was further out into the pasture, we joined him there. As I stood next to him, Pam snapped a photo and then another. It was the third shot that became my favorite. Ollie reared his head up, and with his mouth wide open, his prominent teeth gleaming and his lips open to the sky, he neighed as if laughing.

His silliness was contagious, and I broke out in laughter. The photo of Ollie and me is priceless and reminds me of the importance of play and laughter.

More insight came to me a few days later. I realized when I embrace my own power it's truly the one thing no one can ever take away from me. I also realized that whether I'm in the physical presence of Ollie or not, he is a part of me, just like the animals I've shared my life with and white wolf. Each have guided me, just as surely as nature and the Creator have done.

Horses have known this ancient wisdom all along. The more I let myself be with this, allowing it to integrate, the more I feel all animals are calling us to awaken and live fully in the truth of who we are.

CHAPTER 15

Growing Angst

IT IS COMMONLY said in spiritual circles that we are all a work in progress. I have come to realize and own this truth for myself, and I have witnessed it in others as well. Just when we think we have life figured out we are called to go inward yet again. This time is crucial to our growth and in helping us to live more fulfilling lives. Indeed, the day we stop growing is the day we put a cap on our own infinite potential.

Unfortunately, our culture doesn't seem to put enough value on stillness and the importance of inward reflection and contemplation. Instead, we have been socialized to mask our insecurities or challenges that are too hard to face with overeating, shopping or excessive consumption of alcohol. I can definitely say I've used all three crutches at different times as a way of not facing issues that were bothering me.

But as I've learned to work with my fears, the more I've come to welcome them as mentors trying to show me the way to transform and evolve. This is not always easy, far from it. But when I look back, I can see with clarity the messages I needed to understand.

After my work with Ollie I once again felt confident that I'd healed the pain I'd carried with me all these years, but there was yet more to be revealed. It was something I really didn't see coming.

I started to notice that the more I grew into the next phase of my life—and in a direction I felt excited about—the more uncomfortable I became. In fact, there were many days when, though I didn't think I was showing it outwardly, I felt resentment and anger simmering just below the surface. It was only later, while going through an intense dark period, that this fury showed itself. John, who was the unfortunate witness, wasn't sure how to talk to me about it. We had been married for thirty-four years at that point and he knew me well enough to know that if he tried to broach the subject of my anger—and the reason for it—I would have likely gotten defensive. He would eventually share with me that he sensed I was searching for *something*, though he wasn't sure what it was.

What he may not have known was that in addition to my growing anger and resentment, I was also feeling deep shame and guilt because those feelings were being directed at Gidget.

As I shared at the beginning, Gidget had many health challenges when she came to live with us. These included, as mentioned earlier, the need to have her bladder expressed four or five times a day, as is commonly the case with dogs with mobility issues and IVDD. I also tried to keep her on a poop schedule as well, however, despite my best efforts accidents could and did happen with frustrating regularity, especially overnight.

For the most part, things ran fairly well with Gidget, especially since I worked from home and was able to adhere to a schedule. However, there was a time during the winter of 2018 when I thought I was going to lose my mind.

Incontinent dogs are also prone to urinary tract infections, which are often caused because they can't hold their bowels. Despite my best efforts to express Gidget before bedtime, she was still prone to accidents overnight. I'd often find her sitting in her own feces in the morning, which was especially worrisome because the bacteria from the feces could then enter the vulva and lead to a bladder infection.

Gidget had experienced infections before I adopted her and also had at least one every year since living with us. I'd done my best to avoid this occurring, but it began to feel like all I was doing was cleaning up urine and feces. Frustration continued to build, and there were many days when I burst into tears upon seeing I'd have to clean up yet another accident; this, along with my concern that she would get yet another infection.

I also spent a lot of time mentally beating myself up and telling myself I should have done better. I couldn't bear the idea of Gidget always having to be on antibiotics, especially since these drugs could weaken her immune system over time. There was also the concern that she could become resistant to antibiotic treatment, and how would we treat her bladder infections then?

In mid-January, Gidget ended up with another bladder infection and once again she was put on antibiotics. As was the case with each previous infection, she was feeling better within a day or two of being on the medication and the urine accidents stopped. In keeping with protocol, I continued to give her the medication, fourteen days in total.

One day in early February and three days after I had given Gidget her last pill, I was hosting my monthly women's mastermind group at my house.

At that point the four of us had been meeting for over a year, and what began as an effort to support each other in our entrepreneurial pursuits had morphed into deep meaningful discussions that encompassed both our personal and professional lives. These women had become my soul sisters, and our meetings always left me feeling alive and empowered to continue to live life on my terms.

As we settled into my living room, Gidget appeared at my feet and looked up at me as if to say, "Please pick me up." I grabbed her bed next to the chair and placed it beside me. Because she can sometimes leak and had just gone through a bladder infection, I wanted her to lie on her bed so she wouldn't soil the chair if she had an accident.

At our first meeting we had set up parameters for sharing—we would each get fifteen minutes to talk about what we were working on, or a challenge we were struggling with, while the rest of us listened without interjecting. When we were done sharing we could either ask for feedback or state that we just wished to be heard.

Monica had just started sharing when I realized I smelled urine. Not wanting to disrupt her, I gently lifted Gidget from her bed and noticed a wet spot below her backend; the bed was wet as well. I quietly excused myself, taking her bed with me, so I could go clean Gidget. When I returned, I brought along a bath towel and placed it on my lap so Gidget could still be near me.

Just as I'd settled back into my chair and turned my attention back to Monica, I felt something warm on my arm. I realized Gidget had leaked urine again, even though I had just expressed her moments ago after cleaning her up.

I wiped the urine from my arm with the end of the towel. It was just a few seconds later that a stream of urine shot out from her backend. I could feel my frustration peaking as I tried to hold it together.

"I'm so sorry," I said, "Gidget just finished a round of antibiotics, and I think her bladder infection has returned or didn't entirely clear up the first time."

Before I knew it, this intense angst came spilling out in tears and frustration, just as it had when I was with my mom in December.

I was overwhelmed by what felt like a never-ending battle with Gidget's infections. It didn't help matters any that when the meeting first began Pam, who was also in the group, had mentioned how fun it would be for the four of us to go on a weekend retreat together.

Just a few months earlier, another friend had suggested we attend a retreat hosted by one of our favorite authors, Joan Anderson. It was something I very much wanted to do. I also thought it would be fun to go to a bed and breakfast for a little getaway, which my best friend had often suggested we do.

All of this was racing through my mind, adding to my growing feeling of being trapped. How could I go away, when I was the only one who could express Gidget properly?

"I just don't know what to do for Gidget anymore," I said. "I'm so tired. I'm just so tired."

It wasn't the first time I had felt this way. In fact, the pressure had been building over the last four years. There were many times I yearned for more freedom, but it seemed there was no way out.

"I'm also just so tired of feeling like I can't do the things I want." I turned toward Pam and added, "I'd love to go with all of you for a weekend away, but I just can't and this adds to my frustration."

"Gidget could come with us," Lisa suggested. "We could go somewhere that allows dogs."

Though I loved her for offering, I couldn't deny how I truly felt, even though there was so much shame and guilt that came with it. "I don't want to take Gidget with me. I feel the need to spend some time away from her."

I then realized that Monica hadn't been done sharing and all the attention was on me. "I'm so sorry, Monica. I didn't mean to take away from what you were talking about."

Pam said, "There's no need to feel bad." Everyone nodded in agreement.

She then got up and sat next to Gidget and me. If I wanted, she said, perhaps we could burn some sage and hold space for Gidget and me to heal.

A part of me wanted to do this, but I felt guilty for having taken up too much time already. "No, it's okay. I'm fine now. Please Monica, carry on with what you were sharing. I'm fine, really."

But it wasn't the truth. There was this heaviness inside me, and I didn't know how I was going to lift it anytime soon.

CHAPTER 16

Judgment

IT WAS MID-AFTERNOON when my circle of friends departed. I knew I had to get Gidget to the vet. I called and was able to get her in yet that day. As I drove the fifteen minutes to the next town where the office was located, tears rolled down my cheeks again.

I just didn't know how much longer I could do this. I was concerned that Gidget's infection was back or hadn't gone entirely away. I was also anxious about the cost of yet another office visit, plus procedures or treatment that would be suggested. A heavy burden descended upon me once again.

I walked into the clinic with Gidget in my arms and a towel wrapped around her backend in case she had another accident. The receptionist said it would be a few moments. I took a seat in the waiting area. It was only about a minute later that I felt something warm on my arm. Gidget had leaked again. Just then I saw a vet tech standing before me.

"Hi, Barb and Gidget."

I tried to smile but I just didn't have the energy.

Holding out her arms she said, "I'll take Gidget. I'll bring her to the back so we can extract some urine from her bladder and have it sent off to the lab for a culture."

I handed Gidget over along with the towel. "Just so you know, the towel is wet. She leaked."

"No problem," she said as she took Gidget in her arms and headed to the back of the clinic.

Now sitting alone, my mind became a tornado of worry while my body felt numb. A few moments later Dr. Mary walked out to the waiting area and sat down next to me.

"The technician is getting urine from Gidget right now. We will then send it off to the lab to see what type of bacteria we are dealing with."

I nodded in approval.

"I'm a bit surprised that her infection is back, though it's not uncommon with chronic occurrences for the antibiotic to stop working. We may have to try something stronger, depending on how the culture comes back."

I just nodded again. It seemed I lacked the strength to do anything else.

"I can see you're exhausted," she said.

This surprised me. I thought I was concealing it well. Hesitant, but relieved someone noticed, I said, "Well, actually, yes, I am."

"Barb, I want you to know that no one here would judge you, no matter what decision you'd make for Gidget."

I just looked at her, not knowing what she was getting at.

"You've done ninety-nine percent more than most of our clients would do. It can take a toll when you are dealing with chronic health issues."

I said, "I'm not worried anyone here would judge me."

After I said it, I knew it wasn't the complete truth. There were times I worried people judged the way I cared for Gidget, especially when, as mentioned earlier, it came to my belief about incorporating holistic modalities. Dr. Benner and the others at the vet didn't always understand my approach, which had often left me feeling frustrated, or like I was doing something wrong with regard to Gidget's health.

There were also times when I thought about how much money I'd spent over the years caring for special needs dogs. There were undoubtedly added expenses one doesn't incur with a healthy dog. Often I'd think about those who couldn't afford the treatment for chronic issues and whose only option was to give their pet up or euthanize them. I couldn't imagine having to make that difficult decision.

But I was also questioning how much more I could do for Gidget, or whether it was even fair to keep putting her through all she had endured. There was so much to think about, and Dr. Mary's well-intended but disturbing words had only added to my anxiousness.

She said, "We should know the results of the culture by Monday at the latest, and what the next step is. For now, I'll send you home with more of the same antibiotic I just treated her with so she is comfortable."

"Okay, this sounds good," I said.

She placed her hand on my knee and looked into my eyes. I felt great empathy from her as she said, "Try and take good care of yourself."

"Thank you," I said as she walked away and I waited for the refill of the antibiotics.

CHAPTER 17

Cycle of Confusion

WITHIN A DAY the antibiotics kicked in again. The first sign was that Gidget wasn't leaking as frequently as she had been. While I was happy she was comfortable again, it was also a relief to not have to clean up urine so frequently.

Tried as I might, I couldn't stop thinking about what Dr. Mary had said. It played like a broken record in my head. It consumed me. Though she hadn't used the word euthanize, to me the implication seemed clear. Though it helped ease some of the angst I'd been feeling for a long time and validated that these feelings were normal, it didn't ease my confusion as to the right and best decision for Gidget.

Just after lunch on Monday afternoon, my cell phone rang. It was Dr. Mary.

"The culture came back. The bacteria is E. coli, which means it ascends into the body from the outside."

This confirmed my suspicion that bacteria from Gidget's poop had gotten into her vulva yet again. And, as she was more prone to accidents overnight and her little lady part was more exposed than my other two female doxies, I knew this would continue to be a challenge.

"As I mentioned last week when you brought Gidget in, when we treat chronic issues with the same antibiotic there is always the risk that they will become resistant to it at some point. We then have to try a more potent antibiotic, though there is the possibility that Gidget's system may not tolerate it."

"I see," I said. "What do you think the best course of action is?"

"I've thought about that. I think we should keep Gidget on the same antibiotic. It could be that perhaps it just wasn't long enough to clear things up. If that doesn't work, then we will need to re-evaluate."

"I understand," I said, then paused for a moment. "Well, let's do that then."

"Okay, sounds good. I'll have the technician put another prescription together for you. You can pick it up then when it's convenient."

"Thank you." Taking a deep breath, I said, "There's something I need to understand from our conversation last week. Do you have another minute or two?"

"Yes, of course."

"Well, first of all, I want to thank you for your kindness in recognizing how tired I am. You are right, it has all been weighing heavily on me. When you said that I've done more than what ninety-nine percent of your other clients would do for their pets I was surprised, though I can't say I haven't thought about those who come to a point where they can't emotionally or financially handle it."

My voice began to shake as I took another deep breath. "I want to be clear about what I believe you were trying to say to me. Did you mean that euthanizing Gidget is an option if I feel I can't do this anymore?"

"Yes, that's what I meant. It's not an easy discussion to have with my clients. I don't always bring this up, as you can imagine, because of the sensitive nature. But I've sensed the last few times you've had Gidget in that you are tired and stressed."

"Yes, this is true," I said. "And again I really do appreciate your recognizing this, and your concern."

"Your quality of life is important, too," she said, "and that's why I felt it important to bring it up."

"You know, you couldn't have said that to me with my first disabled dachshund, Frankie. I would have been upset. But now… well, there are days when I just don't know how much more I can take."

I paused for a moment. "I guess I never really thought about my quality of life. Though I have been concerned if I can't get a handle on this that it could lead to physical issues down the road for me. The financial part also weighs on me."

Dr. Mary said, "I understand. It's why I said that no one here at the clinic would judge you if you make that decision."

I was quiet for a moment. "I'm grateful that you could bring this up with me, Dr. Mary. I have a lot to think about. But I do think it's worth giving this next round of antibiotics a shot and then taking it from there."

"Of course," she said. "I'll have that ready for you to pick up."

"Okay, sounds good. I'll pick it up yet today. Thanks again for taking the time to talk with me."

"You're welcome. Take good care and please don't hesitate to call with any questions or concerns."

After we said our goodbyes, I sat on the ottoman in my writing cottage and gazed out the window still filled with some confusion. *Was euthanizing really an option? Could I really do that?* My mind couldn't rest.

I'm fortunate to have a close bond with my mom. There have been countless times when I've turned to her as my trusted confidant to help guide me through troubling times. I knew I needed her now and she'd be there for me.

I sent her a text asking if she was home. She responded right away that she was.

"Can I stop over?" I texted back, "I really need to talk with you."

"I'll be here."

I threw my jacket on and told Gidget I'd be back in a little while, then jumped into my car. Within ten minutes I was standing on my mom's front porch ringing the doorbell. Her dogs Charley and Dolly Jo enthusiastically greeted me when she opened the door, but I was so full of conflicting emotions I didn't engage with them as I usually do.

As we walked down the hall to the kitchen, she said, "Would you like some Chai tea?"

"Yes, I'd really like that." In truth, I could have really gone for a glass of wine, but I wanted my head to be clear as I talked to her.

She set up the machine to brew the tea and I took a seat at the island in the middle of her kitchen.

"It's about Gidget," I began.

"I kind of thought perhaps that's why you wanted to talk."

This didn't surprise me. She knew me well. Besides, I kept her abreast of what was going on in my life.

"I just don't know what to do, Mom. I'm really confused."

"What happened since we last talked?"

I shared all the details regarding the results of the culture and the discussion I'd had with Dr. Mary.

"I've never had these kinds of thoughts before. Is it really in Gidget's best interest to keep treating her with antibiotics, given their potential for weakening her immune system over time?"

She listened as I continued. "I'd never really thought about my quality of life either until Dr. Mary mentioned this to me. You know, how tired I've been feeling. I often question how long I can continue to be there for all of Gidget's needs."

I hesitated for a few moments. "I just don't know if I could put her to sleep. It's such a difficult decision. I'm so confused. And I'm not expecting you to give me an answer as I know there's no easy answer to this. It just sucks."

"You're right," she said. "It's not an easy decision, and it's one only you can make. I know you will do what you feel is best. I have total faith in you."

This is the one of the many things I've always loved and appreciated about my mom. She's never interfered in my life, or those of my siblings, but she's always there to walk beside us during challenging times.

A part of me wanted her to tell me the "right" solution, but I knew in my heart that she was right. Only I could make this decision.

"I know," I said. "I'll figure it out. But no more disabled dogs after Gidget is gone, whenever that is. I just can't do this anymore."

I gave her a hug and thanked her for once again letting me vent and get all my feelings out on the table. I still didn't know exactly how things would shake out, but I felt a little more at peace.

CHAPTER 18

Gidget Speaks

AS I DROVE home with Gidget's latest round of meds, my thoughts turned to the many years I had spent caring for animals. From five cats early on in my married life to Cassie Jo, our sweet chocolate Lab who after a nine-month battle succumbed to terminal bone cancer, to the three disabled dachshunds I had cared for, and Kylie, our yellow English Lab who we said goodbye to in November of 2017. No matter how long they were with us or what their challenges were, their quality of life was forefront in my mind.

It wasn't until recently and everything I was going through with Gidget that I'd begun to question my own quality of life. Looking back, I realize there had been whisperings for some time, but I had been afraid to listen, let alone express these sentiments out loud. I was scared of judgment from others, and especially from the audience I'd built over the years. I thought people would view me as selfish for having these feelings.

The burden I felt in caring for Gidget was real, though. It was also complicated, a vicious cycle of resentment followed by feelings of intense guilt and shame. *How could I be the woman who loved animals deeply, who had built much of her identity on this love, be feeling this way?* These questions ran on a loop, plaguing most of my waking hours. I felt like I was engaged in a great inner battle and that regardless of the outcome I was going to be the loser.

It was while in this midst of this inner turmoil, and shortly after my "mini-breakdown" during the women's circle, that I enrolled in Colette Baron-Reid's Oracle School, specifically the first level course of personal mastery. As mentioned earlier, I had been using oracle cards for years, and during my two-month sabbatical in 2013 I had incorporated coach Cheryl Richardson's Grace card deck with my daily journaling, which helped me tap deeper into my intuition and guide me forward during that tender time.

One of the things that surfaced during that sabbatical was a desire to be of service to women who were feeling stuck and struggling in their lives. Ironically, as I began Colette Baron-Reid's course, I found it was stirring things up in me that weren't always comfortable, things related to my own feelings of "stuckness." I started to see how certain patterns played out in my life. I was understanding that I always had the choice to course correct and move in a different direction.

That said, though there were many aspects of personal mastery that were helping me, my anxiety continued to increase. I awoke one morning near the end of February and had this overwhelming dread that I just didn't want to face the day. It felt like this massive heavy energy was weighing me down. I just didn't want to function.

Slowly I pulled myself up, sat on the edge of the bed and glanced down at Gidget in her kennel. I noticed she'd pooped in there, which both added to my dread and gave me the push I needed to get up. I gently and carefully removed Gidget from her kennel so as to avoid dragging her through the excrement, and whisked her off to the kitchen sink for a bath.

As I ran warm water over her fur and soaped up her tiny body, I could feel tears hovering on the edge, wanting more than anything to bust through. But I kept pushing them down trying to keep them at bay.

I went through the motions of towel-drying Gidget, cleaning out her kennel and tossing her bedding into the washing machine, then collapsed onto the living room sofa. It felt like a dark cloud was overhead and descending faster and faster, ready to swallow me whole. I needed support; the kind of support only Dawn could provide.

Just realizing that I could turn to her brought a sense of relief and with tears streaming down my face I grabbed my iPad and composed an email to her. I didn't expect an immediate response—it was still early and given the three-hour time difference between Wisconsin and Alaska I knew Dawn was most likely still asleep—but just reaching out made me feel better.

A few hours later, Dawn wrote me back. "Is this an emergency? I do have plans for the day but can make time for you if need be. If not, I can talk with you Monday morning."

Tears flowed again as I read her response. I really wanted relief *now*, but I also wanted to respect her time. This wasn't an emergency, not really, so I took a deep breath and trusted that it was meant to be, and the best for all involved, for me to wait a few days.

I wrote back and said Monday would be fine. In the meantime, per Dawn's request, I would take some photos of Gidget and send them to her. She would need those to tune into Gidget's energy on Monday morning.

Though I took some comfort in knowing I'd be talking with Dawn soon, I continued to do battle with my emotions. By the time Saturday morning rolled around, I was tired of feeling sad. I asked myself what I could do to get out of this funk, and within minutes, Lake Michigan and the North Pier popped into my mind.

That was it. I bundled Gidget in her lavender polar fleece coat and strapped her into her dog seat, which was on the front passenger side and perched up high so she could see out the window, then we headed east toward the lake.

There's something about driving country roads that soothes my nerves. It felt good just to be driving and taking in the countryside views, even though it was the middle of winter. When we arrived at North Pier thirty minutes later, I found the one small parking area was full. Not surprisingly, it's a favorite spot to gaze out at the endless water, watch the seagulls and other bird life, and take in the view of the lighthouse as waves crash onto the rocks.

I drove about a half-mile past the full lot, turned around and found a spot to park along the road in front of a tree. There is a walking path between the road and the lake, and many people were out taking advantage of it, though it was only in the upper twenties and quite windy.

I rolled the window halfway down so I could hear the sound of the waves and found their rhythmic crashing to be like a much-needed massage for my weary mind.

We were only sitting there for a few moments when I noticed two cars pull out of the North Pier parking lot, so I quickly put my car in drive and went back to claim a spot. As I gazed out over the blue-green water that looked like it went on forever I felt peace wash over me. Overhead, I saw seagulls flying, along with the occasional duck or two.

"Look Gidget!" I said the first time I saw one, "A duck! Can you believe it?"

Unlatching her from her car seat, I scooped her into my arms and perched her high on my chest. "See all that water out there? Isn't it beautiful?"

It was then I felt the tears come again. "I'm trying so hard, Gidget. Really I am." I hugged her close as we sat in contemplation for a little while longer.

Looking down at her sweet face with her understanding eyes, my heart melted with love for her. I also felt a surge of guilt for not being the most stable person to be around of late. I wanted more than anything for Gidget to know that I truly loved her. I felt bad that she was likely sensing my struggle, though her patience with me was so generous and noble.

I didn't know what my conversation with Dawn would bring, but I felt a little better as Gidget and I headed back home.

Before I knew it Monday morning had arrived and I was sitting face-to-face, via video conference, with Dawn. During my past readings, Dawn usually began by asking what was going on and gathering details so she had some background to work with.

But today she said, "When I tuned into Gidget this morning she had so much to share! So much so I almost couldn't keep up while writing it all down. I'm going to go ahead and share everything I received from her first."

Grabbing my notebook and a pen, I said, "Okay, sounds good."

I had to write quickly as Dawn began conveying to me what she'd received from Gidget. She began with, *I'm fine just the way I am.*

> *I see things sideways, and this is what I'm here to teach you to do. To help you see subtle perspectives you may not consider.*

You are good at hearing me, but not the fullness of what I'm trying to convey.

My body may not be quick, but I am in my wisdom. (This resonated on many levels as I understood Gidget to be wise and had also noticed signs of her slowing down with age).

Others don't always see my full wisdom, but my higher self is coming through.

My invitation to you is to go deep, to see aspects you have not considered, along with fine details, in order to gain a deeper perspective.

I'm fun-loving, a princess, and I know my divine self. (I chuckled out loud to hear Gidget referring to herself in that way, because it was true!)

What I want for you is to not get caught up in the amazement of something as it prevents you from seeing a sideways view as I'm trying to help you see.

You hear things as the intent, but not always the subtext.

I can be a cuddle buddy.

I give you "that look" to help you understand and that there is something deeper there.

I really want for you to understand inner focus and details, which is my final teaching to you. See this as deep and clear before sharing.

I really love you.

It's okay to be gentle and kind, but deep and true, too.

Lastly, Dawn shared it was important for me to know that Gidget and I were meant to be together for both our needs and desires.

I wasn't quite sure what to make of the reading, which was a bit frustrating. A part of me thought perhaps Gidget was getting ready to move on because of her reference to her "final" teaching for me. Yet this wasn't what I was sensed from the reading overall.

I then asked some questions of Dawn, hoping our conversation could bring more clarity.

"I'm not sure what Gidget means about seeing things sideways," I said, "How do I *do* that?"

"Try not to make it so mental. It doesn't have to be a burden. Imagine sideways as a trap door that you slide down—like a funhouse. It's more relaxing than thinking. Be cool. Don't get excited. Like The Fonz from *Happy Days*—he is cool. He didn't need to try to be cool, he just was."

I took in what Dawn was saying as she continued, "Another way to do sideways is to have more fun with Gidget, not always planned, but in the moment."

Recalling what I'd felt called to do with Gidget just two days ago, I told Dawn about our drive to North Point.

"It was fun observing the waves, seagulls, and ducks with Gidget on my lap. It was a special and beautiful bonding time. I'm going to make a point to do things like this with her more often."

Dawn encouraged me not to force it, but to just *allow* it to happen. "Sideways is paying attention to the little things that fit—and doing that will help you to think sideways."

Clearly I had lots to ponder here.

"Maybe there will be a book about Gidget," Dawn offered.

It was validation of a thought I'd had two weeks earlier while driving to meet a friend for lunch. I told Dawn as much, then added that while the thought excited me, I realized I didn't want to put any constraints on it. I just wanted to let it happen and see if it was meant to be.

It felt good to be in this space of *allowing* instead of forcing, which was something I continually needed to practice.

Dawn said, "Perhaps the title would be what Gidget started out with today—*I'm Fine Just the Way I am*.

Something about that sparked a knowing in me as my hand immediately flew to my chest and rested on my heart. I would have to continue to simmer in its full meaning, but something about it felt true and right.

Dawn looked at two of the photos I had taken of Gidget when we went to Lake Michigan on Saturday.

"Gidget's ears look like the Flying Nun," Dawn observed with a smile. "Did you ever watch that program?"

"Oh yes!" I exclaimed, "I loved that show! You know it was Sally Field who played the Flying Nun, right?"

Dawn nodded yes.

"And Sally Field also played Gidget."

"That's right, she did."

"When I adopted Gidget, that's the name she came with. I didn't feel the need to change it, because, well, she is just such a *Gidget*!"

Dawn said, "Do you remember when Sally won her first Oscar and what she said in her acceptance speech?"

"No, I don't recall that."

"She said, 'You like me. You really like me!' Perhaps there is something there for you to ponder…?"

I knew there was truth in this for me. Oh, how I'd struggled for many years, trying to let go of worrying whether or not others liked me or approved of my path in life. I also knew that I had been slowly moving away from that and evolving into the next phase of my journey. Yet there were still moments of fear that others wouldn't understand or agree with who I was becoming. I was afraid they would no longer like me.

As I thanked Dawn for the reading, I still wasn't sure exactly what it all meant. I just knew I had to sit with it, be patient, and allow it to unfold.

CHAPTER 19

Kinship Connection

TWO DAYS AFTER my reading with Dawn, I saw a post on Facebook from my friend Alice. Eddie, her dachshund in a wheelchair, had passed away. While I was sad for Alice's loss, I realized a part of me was envious of her newfound freedom. She no longer had to care for Eddie's special needs.

I had met Alice over eleven years earlier, as were both walking through a large parking garage.

"Are you by chance going to the writing conference?" she asked me.

"Yes, in fact, I am!"

Our meeting was no coincidence. As we became acquainted during the conference we discovered we had much in common, including a love for dachshunds. In no time we were swapping stories about Frankie and Eddie.

When the weekend came to a close, Alice and I agreed to stay in touch, though we wouldn't connect again until I published my first children's book about how Frankie had become paralyzed and persevered. A few years later, Eddie too became paralyzed, and at the same age Frankie had been when she lost the use of her hind legs. Like Frankie, he was fitted with a dog wheelchair.

Alice's life was vastly different than mine. She was raising four children while also caring for a special needs dog, including having to express his bladder, just as I had with my dachshunds.

Those of us in the IVDD community understand the enormity of this commitment and the challenges it can present. It had been rewarding for me to be there for many people going through the same things I had experienced, giving them hope, and providing resources, especially during those first few months after paralysis that can feel so overwhelming.

This one hit close to home, though. While I didn't know Alice well, I had enjoyed reading her humorous Facebook posts about the trials, tribulations and joys of a keeping up with four kids with a sweet but sometimes stubborn wheelie dog as her sidekick.

Now, after living with IVDD for seven years, Eddie was gone. I sent her a message expressing my sympathy over her loss.

She wrote back: "Thanks so much. I know you know about this part of life all too well. The kids and I had a good cry last night. But we are proud and happy that we helped Eddie see fourteen years. We also talked about his spirit last night as I shared with the kids your post about Gidget possibly communing with Kylie in spirit."

Two weeks after Kylie's passing I'd gotten a sense that perhaps Gidget was picking up on her presence. I had written about it in a recent blog post.

> *I must admit that I feel more in tune with Gidget these days since Kylie passed on. While in some ways I'd love a house full of dogs, I am enjoying this more intimate one to one experience. We have no plans to bring another dog into our lives. We will likely be a one dog household from now on for various reasons.*
>
> *My attention span is no longer split between two dogs. I've had more time now to observe Gidget. I'm enjoying this along with the fact it has been piquing my curiosity about certain aspects of her behavior.*
>
> *Recently I've noticed her lying on the rug between our living room and kitchen, which she hadn't done before. But now, I'm finding her there often. It was a place that Kylie often laid. It wasn't always the best place for a 75-pound dog to lie, as it was a high traffic area of our house. But we also didn't want to disturb Kylie as she seemed so content there, and we just carefully walked around her.*
>
> *What's also interesting is that Kylie had chosen this spot to hang out within the last year of her life. Why she decided to lie in that spot*

> *I wasn't quite sure. It wasn't a place I'd find Gidget hanging out with Kylie or even if Kylie was lying elsewhere. But now I was observing her there often.*
>
> *The last year of Kylie's life John and I would also often find Gidget and Kylie snuggled together in Kylie's kennel. This was new also and it wasn't something they'd done the three years prior since Gidget had come to live with us.*
>
> *Gidget lying in the spot Kylie used to lay, I sensed that perhaps they were communicating in their own unique way. I believe that Kylie knew she was going to be moving on soon and that Gidget was also aware of this. It was a special thing to witness as they deepened their bond. It warmed my heart.*
>
> *With Gidget taking up residence on the rug exactly where Kylie rested most days the last year of her life, perhaps she felt connected to Kylie. While I couldn't say for sure, it's definitely something I strongly sensed. It brings me comfort to know that maybe this is Gidget's way in which she is still communicating with Kylie.*
>
> *We also still have Kylie's huge kennel that resides in part of the kitchen. I'd considered donating it, but I couldn't part with it yet because Gidget had now taken up residence in it. She seems to be enjoying it as her comforting and safe place to be when we are gone.*

Knowing Alice had shared my blog post with her children endeared her to me even more.

We continued to exchange private Facebook messages—she wrote about how she missed Eddie, and I told her some of what I was experiencing with Gidget—and quickly realized we had so much more to share. We agreed to meet for lunch a week later and, as we lived an hour away from each other, chose a restaurant halfway between our homes.

Though there was an undeniable kinship between us, Alice and I had only seen each other in person twice before, most recently at the grand opening of Bookworm Gardens—a children's story garden in my area, where Frankie's story and a statue of her resides.

Now, as we walked side-by-side to the entrance of the restaurant, I felt a bit awkward and sensed she did too. But the moment we were seated inside in a booth and gave the waitress our drink orders the words began to flow easily.

"How are you doing since Eddie has been gone?" I asked.

Alice's eyes filled with tears. She shared with me that she and her husband had planned to put Eddie to sleep six months ago, as he had begun declining quickly toward the end of the summer and stopped eating. They had set the date with the veterinarian and she had prepared her kids as best she could, but her husband started having second thoughts.

In a last-ditch effort, he had rushed Eddie to the ER, where the vet prescribed an appetite stimulant.

"The stimulant helped somewhat, but it also caused Eddie to have diarrhea," Alice told me, "which I had to clean up as I was the one who was home with him. He also continued to decline."

The waitress was back with our drinks and we realized we'd not looked at the menu yet. I told her we needed a few more minutes.

Alice continued to tell me about the pain of watching Eddie slow down, day after day, over six months. Eventually he stopped enjoying or being interested in many of the things he had before.

She told me how torn she had felt, and how concerned she was that Eddie was suffering. She was also coming to the realization that her husband wasn't going to go through with what they had decided.

Tears ran down her face as she told me she had consulted with a vet specializing in hospice care. That conversation confirmed what she already knew, and though she didn't want to make the decision without her husband's consent felt she didn't have a choice. She made the appointment to euthanize Eddie while her husband was out of town on business and her kids were in school. Even though she felt a tremendous amount of guilt, she felt it was something she had to do.

"When I kissed Eddie for the last time, knowing this was finally it, I realized there wasn't much left to lose. In truth I believed we had lost his spirit back in September, and it only continued to get worse. He loved playing with wrapping paper at Christmas but this year he had no interest and walked away. I got him his favorite treats for his birthday, but he wanted nothing to do with them. For the pup who always loved food, it had become challenging to get him to eat even one meal a day."

Eddie had also had Cushing's disease, and the meds were no longer managing his symptoms. Recently his thirst had increased, but his urine output didn't match what he was taking in, which led Alice to believe his kidneys were failing.

"So while I'm sad and I miss him," she said, wiping her tears, "I'm glad he's free from his failing body."

My tears were welling up as well, and this is how the waitress found us when she returned again to take our order. Not wanting to send her away again, we quickly glanced at our menu and chose something to eat.

"Thank you again for all your help and support all these years," Alice said, "Now that I don't have to take care of Eddie twenty-four-seven I plan to get back to writing."

As I listened to Alice and murmured words of understanding, I felt a familiar feeling tugging at my heart. It was the guilt I'd felt when I first read of Eddie's passing and found myself envious that she would now have more time for herself. But I took comfort in the fact that she expressed her desire to get back to something she enjoyed.

"Have you had any other signs that Gidget is communicating with Kylie?" Alice asked.

"No, I haven't sensed anything since I wrote that blog post," I replied, "But I have had a lot going on with Gidget."

I had eluded to some inner turmoil during our Facebook chat the week before, but now I felt comfortable to share more about what I was going through. Now it was Alice's turn to listen as I spoke of my feeling of overwhelm and despair with regard to taking care of Gidget. I also told her about my session with Dawn.

"After talking to her I felt like a cloud had lifted, and that I was moving in the right direction, but since then things have only gotten more intense."

I told her that though Gidget was in good spirits and loved to eat, she had chronic UTIs. I also told her how exhausted I was with the constant demands of caring for her. At some point the waitress brought our food, though we were both too engrossed in our conversation to eat much.

"Once Gidget transitions I don't think I'll be adopting another special needs dachshund. While I'd love another dog at some point, I plan to take a break. I also don't know if I'd get another wiener dog. I just don't want to deal with the possibility of another IVDD diagnosis, and all that it entails."

That was hard to say, and still is, because dachshunds are my favorite breed. But the reality is that one in four are diagnosed with disc disease and as of now there is no cure.

I then shifted to a more positive note. "I do believe a book may come out of this dark period, and I've even started jotting down some notes and insights that might go into it. Mostly, though, I'm just trying to be open and see where life takes me."

I paused for a moment as I thought about the timing of Eddie's passing. It wasn't an accident that I had met Alice at a writing conference and then supported her during a challenging time when Eddie became paralyzed. Now the roles were reversed as I shared similar struggles and feelings of being unable to cope.

"I can't help but think that though it's under sad circumstances reconnecting with you now is divine timing, as I'm in this unknown space right now with Gidget and myself."

Alice nodded her understanding. "We won't be getting another pet for some time either. I feel we need to focus on our family and ourselves now. I was trying to think of the best word to describe the past eight years and *constrained* came to mind."

"Thank you for your honesty, Alice. I've been moving through similar emotions myself. I often describe it as feeling trapped—and resentful—which as you know is hard to admit. I'm eternally grateful for all that my special needs dogs have taught me, but I'm feeling ready to experience life in a new way someday."

"I'm also glad that I got to experience all I did with Eddie. He not only helped me but also my kids. There were many beautiful lessons they learned growing up with a disabled dog. But there were times when it was hard for them to understand. Now they will get to experience life without those constraints.

"For myself, I feel like those years were about self-denial. While I believe there is a season for everything, this is now the season for more self-care and honoring the personal needs I set aside for all those years."

It was like she was taking the words right out of my mouth. "It's so comforting to hear you say all of this, Alice. These feelings have been hard for me to process at times, and to own them."

In that moment, I realized that in writing a book about this leg of my journey I might be able to help others, just as Alice was helping me. I said as much to her, then half-jokingly added, "But why does it have to be so painful?"

We both smiled.

"I've been trying to find someone who I can talk with about my feelings. There has to be someone out there who can help," I said.

I admitted to Alice that what I was really struggling with was resentment and anger. "It's difficult to have these feelings of resentment toward this little being I love so much. How can I be this advocate for special needs dogs while also desperately wishing to be free?"

Alice nodded in understanding.

"I've also begun to question whether Gidget is suffering. Is it fair to have her leaking overnight, sitting in her own urine and feces? Not to mention the times she 'cleans' it up herself by eating it. Is that really a quality of life for her?"

On the other hand, I wrestled with the question of whether this was cause for putting her to sleep. Throughout my years of advocating on behalf of paralyzed dogs I had often said, "We wouldn't think of putting a human who needs the aid of a wheelchair to sleep, so why would we think that for a dog?" Frankie and Joie had thrived in a wheelchair, though I realized a wheelchair wasn't for every dog. Each situation had to be carefully looked at to determine what was best for that particular animal.

This led to a discussion about death.

Alice had been a nurse for many years; it was how she had met her husband, who is a doctor. She talked about his training, and that his understanding was to "fix" a patient that wasn't well. This, Alice observed, had carried over into his treatment of Eddie, including his decision to take Eddie to the ER and in using the prescribed appetite stimulant. Alice, on the other hand, had felt Eddie was suffering and didn't feel right about trying to force him to eat with a medication.

We both agreed that her husband's approach, while well-intentioned, was part of a larger societal issue around how we think of death. Indeed, even talking about it often seemed taboo.

"This is where I feel confused," I said, "How do I know that Gidget isn't suffering? With my other dogs I was beside myself with worry about the day I would have to put them to sleep, and I grieved so deeply when they passed. Now I feel like I have a different perspective.

"I'll be sad and miss Gidget when she moves on, but I've also come to know that she, and all my dogs before her, are part of me. They always will be. I can never lose that. Being in the world of dogs all these years, there were times when I'd question silently whether someone was doing the 'right' thing for their pet. This was more of an observation than a judgment, though to be honest there have been times when I wondered if an animal was suffering because their human couldn't bear to let them go. It tears at my heart when I see and feel this."

We then talked about how many humans also endure suffering, how they are kept alive by drugs and other artificial means because as a society we find it difficult to accept death. This suffering was even more unnecessary with pets because we have euthanasia as an option.

Alice and I understood that there wasn't an easy or right answer to any of this, and our experiences with our pets hadn't made it any easier. While it was comforting to share these feelings with each other, the conversation seemed to leave us with even more questions to consider.

"It was difficult as a nurse to know a patient was suffering," Alice said, "and I felt the same way about Eddie. It has me thinking of perhaps someday training to become a death doula."

My friend Marggie is a death doula and had told me much about this sacred work of assisting those in the dying process and supporting their families. What stuck with me most, however, was her observation that the people who struggle most with leaving this earth are those who have not made peace with their lives.

Again I thought about our ability to end our pets' suffering. Was it right to interfere with their journey, or should we allow it to be a natural process, as it was with people? Though I sometimes leaned toward the latter, I didn't feel I could trust myself to go through this with my own pets.

Our conversation then turned back to quality of life, this time my own. "I feel selfish for wanting my freedom, and at the same time I'm trying to balance that with wanting to do what is best and right for Gidget."

My eyes filled with tears as guilt once again rose to the surface. "I really do love Gidget," I said as I met Alice's eyes and saw hers were brimming as well.

"I completely understand what you are saying, Barb."

We sat there for a few moments in silence. Two women who had walked similar journeys and understood the depth of what each other was feeling, separate but together.

We could have talked well into the next day and then some, but Alice needed to pick her youngest daughter up from kindergarten. We agreed to stay in touch. We now felt more connected than ever because of what we had so honestly shared during our time together.

I still didn't have clarity, but I didn't feel as alone anymore. Talking with Alice helped to lighten some of the burden I was carrying in my heart.

CHAPTER 20

Personal Mastery

THE CONVERSATION WITH Alice and the reading with Dawn continued to evoke many emotions. What I didn't realize at the time, however, was that I was descending into a dark hole.

Indeed, though I'd certainly done my fair share of personal growth work over the past thirteen years, as I now moved through the personal mastery course the truth of the credo "We are always a work in progress" was more apparent than ever.

My work now was to try to let go of blame, shame, and victim mentality, and I was slowly coming to a new place of awareness. Though I had used oracle cards before, taking part in this course was helping me to go even deeper in dialogue with myself. It was helping me to understand and shift my perspective of how unaddressed wounds can cause us to suffer needlessly and repeat patterns that keep us stuck in old ways of thinking.

As I began to work with Colette Baron-Reid's *Wisdom of the Oracle* deck, I began to see the cards as reflections of what it was I needed to look at, just as my dogs had been reflections for me over the years. The cards were gently guiding me to open to what may be the root cause of my recent challenges.

At times it was difficult and painful. But the more I learned to be an observer of myself and let judgment go, the more insight I was able to gain about why I behaved in certain ways.

One of the reasons I was attracted to Colette's teachings and her Oracle School was the emphasis on personal growth. Colette's philosophy is based on that of Socrates and holds great reverence for the Temple of Apollo at Delphi, an ancient Greek religious sanctuary with the inscription "Know Thyself" over the doorway. This resonated with me, much like the words of Taoist philosopher Lao Tzu: "Mastering others is strength. Mastering yourself is true power."

During the second week of personal mastery we were invited to do a *Becoming* reading. We were given a series of self-inquiry questions, then asked to pick a card for each question and ponder the meaning. One by one I wrote the questions in my journal and pulled an oracle card for each.

The first question asked us to determine which part of ourselves needed the most healing. Now, as I look back on this question, and in rereading the journal I kept, I'm taken to a more-in-depth understanding of the power of the card I drew. It was *Never-ending Story*.

The essential meaning of the card speaks to our wounded ego, the endless self-criticism, and the unnecessary drama this can create. The oracle's message reads:

> *"There is a story woven through the imperfect fabric of life that tells of hurt and loss, rejection and humiliation, self-loathing and arrogance, and all manner of suffering born of unnecessary dramas. It is the old story whose refrain is that you cannot do this, must not go there, should not say that—lest your world come crumbling down. Today, know that none of this is actually true. The sky is not falling. The voice you hear is just a small, scared, conditioned part of you that got stuck in life, wants to protect you, and needs to be seen as a victim. Love that piece of you. Fear is all it knows. Distorted guidance is preventing you from being true to yourself. You are not your story, and the narrator is simply the voice of your fearful part, small and vulnerable and easily soothed."*

In my journal, I wrote down what resonated personally for me, which in all honesty, was *every word*. As I did I was filled with a mix of emotions, frustration chief among them. I was so tired of trying to "figure myself out." I wrote about how often I didn't feel good enough or smart enough, and how I had this perception that others judged me.

I'd certainly made great leaps of progress in this department, but there were still plenty of times I fell back into old patterning—loathing myself and waging that epic inner battle that had been a part of my life for as long as I could remember.

Digging deeper, I wrote about the little girl in me who had wounds she was still trying to make sense of and work through. I realized that this little girl was afraid, and that, oddly enough, my self-criticism was a way of protecting her from experiencing further hurt. While I understood this on one level, I knew I still had much work to do in order to fully integrate it. Part of this work was incorporating Colette's teaching to live within a twenty-four-hour compartment, as a way of not getting caught in the cycle of dwelling in the past or projecting too far into the future.

We initially began with pulling one card a day, then eventually moved to three. Card one was the "anchor," addressing the dominant energy around the question or challenge we were working on. The second card suggested the next right action step, and the third showed the potential outcome if we took that suggested action.

As I worked with the various questions and cards, I was learning to further open to and trust my own inner oracle. This was helping me to *lead* my life, instead of running on the "autopilot" of old patterns.

The more I began to understand myself through working with oracle cards, the more I became intrigued as to how I might eventually guide other women to explore what their souls wanted and how they too could begin to live more meaningful lives. Since then I have offered readings online to clients who want to do the deeper inner work these cards evoke.

It wasn't always easy to go beneath the surface to excavate difficult emotions, but I was committed. I was also looking forward to the vacation John and I had planned for mid-March. It would be a nice reprieve from the inner work I was doing.

CHAPTER 21

Second Chances

IN HIS TWENTY-FIVE-PLUS years as a General Contractor, John had found that late fall or early spring was the best times for us to get away. While I preferred the fall, this time John wanted to head somewhere warm and leave behind the cold and snow of Wisconsin. As the time drew near, I became more and more excited about hitting the road in our camper.

In its former life, the camper had been one of two Chevy cargo vans John used for his work. When a few years earlier his last employee set out on his own, John decided he too would go solo and thus would only need one van. He had converted the other into a vehicle for us to use on vacations.

Like many, when the economy tanked in 2008, we had to make some tough financial decisions. While they were difficult, I don't regret these choices because they felt right for us. They had, however, left us feeling that we wouldn't be doing much traveling, if any, in the future. When John had the idea of converting his work van, we enthusiastically embraced it. This would be our ticket to respites, exploration, and inspiration in places far from home.

During its transformation John had taken to call it "The Vamper"; then, the summer before we were to take it out on its first official outing I brought up the idea of giving our van another name.

At the time I was reading *Together, Alone: A Memoir of Marriage and Place*, Susan Wittig Albert's memoir about her marriage at mid-life to a man named Bill. Susan and Bill were both writers and worked from home—something Susan had been yearning to do for a few years before leaving her job at a university.

They also found themselves craving space and a place to settle down that was far away from the hustle and bustle of the modern world. Eventually Susan and Bill moved to a piece of land in Texas he had bought years before; they built a home and named the many beautiful acres that surrounded it *Meadow Knoll*. They would spend many years there, growing their own food and raising animals, as well as working on their various writing projects.

Before settling at *Meadow Knoll*, they had lived and traveled in an RV, which they'd named *Amazing Grace*. I thought that was absolutely beautiful! I imagined the many places they'd visited and all the sunsets and sunrises, mountains and oceans they had seen. I also had no doubt that when in the splendor of nature and traversing the countryside, they had experienced many moments that could be defined as "amazing grace."

In an effort to entice John to rename our van, I asked If I could read a few passages from *Together, Alone* to him.

"Okay," he said, though he didn't sound all that enthusiastic.

I read him the section on how Susan came to name their RV. When I was done, he chuckled. "So that's where you came up with the idea of naming our van!"

Embarrassed but undeterred, I said, "I thought maybe we could name our van *Freedom*."

"That sounds like something from the free-spirited days of the sixties."

Frustrated and a little hurt by his response, I stood up and quietly walked into the house to refresh my drink. Perhaps, I thought, it was a stupid idea. When I came back outside and sat down, John surprised me.

"How about we name the van *Second Chance*?"

I didn't hesitate. "It's perfect! I love it," I squealed. But more than that, I was thrilled he had understood what I was trying to convey. Indeed, the van was a "second chance" to follow dreams we had thought were lost but could now reclaim in a different way.

Our first trip in Second Chance was to Tennessee, though we didn't stay in it the whole time we were gone. Instead we did a "test run," staying in it one night down and one night back. The other seven days we stayed in a cabin along a river. We were traveling with Kylie and Gidget at the time and felt Kylie would be more comfortable in a cabin for the majority of the vacation.

Now here we were again, ready to take Second Chance for another adventurous spin, this time to South Carolina, though we had plans to visit a few cities in North Carolina as well.

John had really outdone himself in utilizing Second Chance's eighty-four square feet. There were two custom bunk beds and two vertical rows of pull-out plastic bins at the backend of the van which were accessible by opening the back doors, as well as four cubby holes in the cab for additional storage. It was also equipped with a small refrigerator, two solar panels on the roof that generate electricity, and a heating and cooling system. The only thing we didn't have yet was a kitchen.

After extensive research, we bought a Vango Drive-away® tent, which attached to the side of the van and served as extra space or, as in our case, a kitchen area. When we wanted to leave the campground all we had to do is remove the vinyl strip above the top side doors, leaving the tent to stand on its own until we returned.

We also purchased a portable all-in-one stove and oven unit. This could be used inside the van if need be or set up in the tent. Other standard items like a small coffee pot, utensils, dishes, and so on I packed into three large rectangular plastic containers.

It was a tight squeeze, especially with Gidget's kennel. Its positioning, we'd soon come to realize as we stopped along the way to our destination, caused somewhat of a hassle. We'd have to pull many of the containers out of the van and rearrange them each time we stopped for the night. We knew though that once we settled at a campground in South Carolina the extra shuffling around would end. We would also be able to set up the tent, thereby extending our living space so we could set up our temporary kitchen and overflow.

We arrived late afternoon at the campground to bright rays of sunshine and temperatures in the upper seventies. This was a relief, as the week before the weather predictions had included unseasonably cool temperatures. We had even discussed postponing our trip until the end of the month but finally decided to trust and have faith that everything would work out in our favor. Rain was expected the next afternoon and the temperatures expected to drop, but in the meantime I soaked in the warm sunshine beating down on my face as we set up camp.

The next morning, lying in my bunk, I looked through the fan above that circulates air in and out of the van. I could see the trees reaching toward the blue sky with a few wispy clouds floating by. After what felt like an eternity of working to understand my internal challenges, it felt good just to let go and be.

True to the forecast, a severe thunderstorm and tornado watch was issued, and while thankfully there were no tornadoes, the rain came down in buckets! That's when John and I realized there was a detail we had not considered when debating when to continue on with our trip: the noise rain makes on a metal roof. The sound of each drop was magnified and echoed within the cab. Along with the thunder that rumbled often and the flashes of lightning that lit up the sky, it made it difficult to sleep.

It was a long night, but we were grateful we made it through the storms. As we stepped from the van the next morning, we saw the new rug we had purchased the day before and placed outside the van doors to catch dirt was drenched. And, as we were parked on red clay, it had also turned the rug a putrid brown. Blah! It was a mess.

Not a good way to start our second day of vacation. As I felt frustration rising within me, I thought about something my mom often says: "This too shall pass." Indeed, the weather turned out to be quite pleasant, with temperatures in the mid-sixties, and we ended up having a fun day of sightseeing.

We kept an ear to the weather station as we sat around the campfire after dinner and heard that temperatures were expected to drop to the low thirties overnight. This was *way* below average for the area. The extended forecast didn't look good either. More rain was expected and a high temperature in the low fifties, which was an improvement but still unseasonably cool. Lucky for us we had a van! We made the decision to pull up stakes and head somewhere warmer.

The next morning our tent was still damp from the heavy storms that had arrived the night before along with a fierce wind. The wet, clay-stained rug, which had never had time to dry, was now stiff and frozen. The strong winds meant it was going to be a challenge to pack up camp, especially taking the tent down.

I could feel my frustration rising again, though I tried to hold it in while also feeling hopeful we'd soon be somewhere warmer. *This too shall pass*, I repeated in my mind, *This too shall pass.*

I packed up the inside of the van and secured things so they wouldn't fly around while traveling, all the while trying to comfort Gidget, who was anxious, pacing and whimpering. I tried holding her and talking with her but I also needed to keep on task so we could hit the road sooner rather than later. Nothing seemed to ease her distress, and I fought even harder to keep my own emotions in check.

With everything ready to go, it was now time to take the tent down. The wind was raw, and the ropes tied to the tent stakes were shaking wildly. I just wanted warmth and comfort. The tears I'd been trying to hold back finally burst forth.

"Why don't you start the van," John suggested, "You and Gidget can warm up while I work on taking the tent down."

Scooping Gidget into my arms, I jumped in the driver's seat and started the ignition, then crawled over to the passenger side, where I wrapped a blanket around Gidget and held her against my chest. I watched as John wrangled the cold and damp tent in the winds.

As the van began to warm up, some of the tension eased from my body. The more relaxed I became, I realized Gidget was settling down also. But then guilt set in because John was out in the frigid, windy weather and I was snug and warm inside.

When he got the tent down, I hopped out of the van and helped him roll it up. Once the tent was back in the bag and everything was secure inside and outside the van, I felt hope return once again. I also silently told myself that I would make the best of the remainder of the trip, no matter what.

After all, we were heading further south, where we would likely find warmer weather. Most importantly, we were riding in Second Chance which allowed us the flexibility and opportunity to pick up and go as we wished.

CHAPTER 22

Reaching Out

AS WE DROVE down the highway toward North Carolina I tried to stay positive and focus on our vacation. But at times my mind drifted back to the stress I felt regarding Gidget. I worried about what the future held.

I recalled when Frankie first became paralyzed. Our lives, including the way we vacationed, completely changed due to her need to have her bladder expressed. We were now doing the same with Gidget, as I still had not been able to find a pet sitter who was willing to express a dog's bladder four to five times a day. The difference was, it hadn't bothered me when Frankie traveled with us, whereas I now found myself wishing John and I could take a vacation by ourselves.

Even before we left on the trip, stress had started to build. Gidget was finishing up a second round of antibiotics for her latest UTI and I was worried that it might return while we were away. What if I couldn't find a vet who could treat her so many miles from home?

I was so concerned that I spoke to Dr. Mary and we decided to keep her on the medication until we returned so we didn't end up in an emergency situation while on the road.

A short while later the vet tech had called to let me know the additional antibiotic supply was ready for pick-up.

"Just so you know, it's not inexpensive," she said, "It will be one hundred-thirteen dollars."

"I know," I said. "It's okay. I'll pick it up later today."

I didn't say anything to the technician, but it wasn't exactly *okay*. To date, the appointments with Dr. Mary, the medications and testing, and a trip to the holistic vet who suggested a Chinese herb in the hopes it would prevent future infections, added up to nine-hundred dollars. I hated the fact that money was a concern, but it was. I reminded myself that all I could do was take one day at a time. For now, I could rest somewhat knowing Gidget was on the antibiotics. I knew we would re-evaluate once we returned from vacation.

As I mentioned earlier, though I was wrestling internally with many different emotions, I didn't realize that I was exuding a negative energy. I would later learn that John was feeling and witnessing my struggle but didn't approach me for fear that I would get defensive. I agree that was probably an accurate assessment, which is ironic because at the time I felt incredibly alone in my pain and in theory would have been comforted to know that he was silently supporting me.

In North Carolina the weather was predicted to be in the low sixties, but the next day we were met by winds and rain mixed with snow. Two days later we packed up again, this time headed for Greensboro, Georgia. We laughed as we flew down the highway because visiting Georgia was never part of our initial plan. It would turn out to be the best part of our trip.

The temperature was a blessed high sixties as we put down stakes at another KOA campground. The campground had many rolling hills and looked out over Lake Oconee. After we had set up camp we walked down to the lakefront to watch the sunset. As we sat on a picnic table along the shoreline, tears of joy came to the surface. The anxiousness I'd been feeling began to melt away.

The campground's location was ideal. Greensboro was twenty minutes in one direction and Madison, a small town we visited, was twenty minutes in the other. Both areas were eclectic, artsy and charming, and we thoroughly enjoyed exploring and taking in their quaintness.

Just as we'd found a comfortable groove and truly began to relax, it was time to pack up once again and begin the two-day trip back home.

That morning, before we headed out, I was prepping Gidget's food with her meds and herbs when John said, "Gidget sure is a lot of work, isn't she?"

Though I just smiled in response, the comment surprised me. John had watched me care for Gidget, not to mention the dogs who had come before her, for years, yet this was the first time he'd mentioned it. Had he not noticed before the daily routine I had with her? Or with our other dogs? While the thought upset me, I also took some comfort in his acknowledgment.

I was grateful to get away for ten days, but the truth was I didn't feel rested when we arrived home. A part of me continued to yearn for time away without a dog to care for. I also didn't know what would happen once Gidget finished the last round of antibiotics, and this continued to weigh on me.

As we settled back into our routines, I was happy to be in my cozy home once again and began to do more research online. I kept hearing this inner whisper that I really needed more support and to find someone I could talk to regarding the feelings I was experiencing.

It had popped into my mind that perhaps Joe Dwyer might be able to help me. I'd met him online years earlier when I published my first children's book and we had connected over our mutual love of dogs. I'd eventually write a review for *Shelby's Grace*, his book about the pit bull and therapy dog who had helped him with his anxiety and depression. But as quickly as I thought of reaching out to Joe, I dismissed the idea. Given his strong animal advocacy, I worried he may not understand my feelings, or worse, judge me for having them.

So I continued my search. It wasn't easy to find resources for those dealing with the emotions I was feeling. There were countless counselors for people who felt burdened by caring for ill friends and family, so shouldn't there be the same for people dealing with feeling fatigued caring for chronically ill pets?

Eventually, I came across a website called *The Association for Pet Loss and Bereavement* (APLB). It's an organization of volunteers professionally trained in pet bereavement counseling. As I looked around their site and read more about them, I wasn't sure they were a good fit. But I decided to fill out their contact form anyway and at least hear what they had to say.

Two days later, I heard from a woman within the organization. Something about her email didn't feel right to me, but as I hadn't found any other resources, I decided to go back to the APLB website and have another look around. When I clicked on the Board of Directors tab, my eyes widened in surprise. Their treasurer was none other than Joe Dwyer!

As I've mentioned, I wholeheartedly believe in signs from the Universe though I don't always pay attention. In fact, I have joked that at times I need to be hit over the head with a two-by-four until I get it. Now, as I stared at his name on my screen, I wondered, *was Joe really the person I should be contacting?* I decided to click over to his website, where I was reminded of his work as an animal chaplain. Even though I was nervous, it felt like confirmation that contacting him was the right thing to do.

I was at my desk in my writing cottage composing an email to Joe when I heard a loud crash. It sounded like something had fallen outside the cottage, but when I walked to the window and glanced out onto the deck I saw nothing out of place.

I went over to the door, opened it and peered out to scan the deck, but again, I didn't see anything out of the ordinary. I thought perhaps my imagination was working overtime so I sat back down to finish writing Joe.

My hand was shaking as I hit send and the message left my outbox, but once I did it I felt some relief too. Now all I could do was wait for Joe's response—and his reaction.

My thoughts returned to the noise I'd heard a few moments earlier, and I went back to the window, where another peek revealed absolutely nothing amiss.

I had taken a step back toward my desk when I realized what had happened. Several decorative pieces I keep on the windowsill had fallen to the floor. How odd, I thought, what could have caused that? I didn't have the window open and the ceiling fan was off. The cottage was completely still.

I began picking up the pieces that had fallen to the floor and placing them back on the window ledge. There was a miniature stone totem of a wolf, a painted wooden piece, made by a local artist, of two pine trees with a moon peeking out from behind them, a 3D postcard of a wolf, and a laminated quote of a Cherokee Legend.

I stared down at the quote, which I was unable to read without my glasses, and recalled the guided meditation Pam had taken me on during our last coaching session three years prior. It was during that visualization that I had met Laiola, the white wolf that advised me to keep my heart open.

I had not read the Cherokee quote in quite some time, but now I grabbed my readers, suddenly eager to revisit it.

Two Wolves

An old Cherokee is teaching his grandson about life.

"A fight is going on inside me," he said to the boy.

"It is a terrible fight, and it is between two wolves. One is evil—he is anger, envy, sorrow, regret, greed, arrogance, self-pity, guilt, resentment, inferiority, lies, false pride, superiority, and ego.

"The other is good—he is joy, peace, love, hope, serenity, humility, kindness, benevolence, empathy, generosity, truth, compassion, and faith. The same fight is going on inside you—and inside every other person, too."

The grandson thought about it for a minute and then asked his grandfather, "Which wolf will win?"

The old Cherokee simply replied, "The one you feed."

Tears sprang to my eyes, for in the legend of the two wolves I recognized my own struggle. Yes, I had tried hard to push away my wolf of resentment, anger, and guilt, but I had fed it too.

Though it was painful to realize this about myself, I also knew from the core of my being that I had just received a sign from Spirit. It wasn't a coincidence that those items had fallen to the floor as I was emailing Joe. Spirit was confirming for me that I was taking a step in the right direction. I needed support in order to tame what I perceived as the "evil wolf"—that part of me that fought daily with feelings that were especially uncomfortable and unfamiliar. I'd been afraid to really look at *the why* that kept the daily battle going, which had only fed the intensity.

With this sign from Spirit, though I knew it wouldn't be easy, I was more than ready to face my feelings.

Walking back to my computer, I noticed I received a response from Joe. Wow, that was fast, I thought. As soon as I opened the email, I was immediately filled with relief. Joe had expressed concern and said he was more than willing to speak with me to see if he could help.

Two days later, we were on the phone.

CHAPTER 23

Talking to Joe

JOE LISTENED WITHOUT interruption. Because he knew of my previous work with Frankie, he understood the passion I had for my mission at that beautiful time in my life. Since I had not spoken with him in quite a few years, I began with how I was currently feeling and what I felt had led me to this dark place.

"What I'm having a hard time with are these feelings I've never felt before. When Frankie passed, there was no doubt in my mind that I wanted another dachshund with IVDD to care for. When I adopted Joie, I thought I would carry on the work with her as I did with Frankie. I was also aware that I was ignoring a voice within me that wanted to move on, but I was too scared of what others would think. When Joie passed ten months after I'd adopted her, while I didn't initially realize it, I came to understand her passing was all part of a bigger plan."

I told Joe about the inward niggle I'd been feeling for quite some time that I needed to take time for myself, to move inward and focus on what it was I really wanted next. I told him that Joie's passing was what led me to temporarily walk away from my work, and that during that break I had come to realize that Joie's gift to me, and why she couldn't stay, was so I'd begin to understand the gifts within a transitional period of one's life.

I told him how I'd realized I still wanted another disabled dachshund, but this one would be just for me, meaning I wouldn't carry on the work I had done with Frankie and attempted to do with Joie.

I then told him about the joy of finding Gidget on Petfinder.com, as well as the subsequent challenges of the adoption process and the worry that it might not go through. I told him about the early health challenges after the adoption, including the false diagnosis that Gidget had a weak heart, followed by a wonderful year that ended when Gidget started have seizures. This had been the beginning of a years-long roller coaster ride.

"Gidget has had at least one bladder infection each year since I've had her. Most recently, she's had infections back-to-back."

I paused and let out a big sigh. "I'm just so tired, Joe."

"I can certainly understand your feeling this way," he said empathetically, "It sounds like you've been through a lot."

"And to be completely honest, there's the financial part of it too," I said. "So far just this latest round of bladder infections has cost over nine-hundred dollars. I'm at this place of questioning, when is enough, enough?"

I shared how I was struggling and questioning whether or not this was really a quality of life for Gidget. "Do I continue to put her through having a needle inserted into her bladder every time she has an infection, not to mention the antibiotics and herbs she has to take? If I was her, I don't even know if I'd want to eat my food with all those herbs and medications piled on top. Is it really fair to her? I just don't know."

Joe asked me more about the many feelings I was having and whether I was willing to examine where they may possibly be coming from.

Though I wanted to say yes, it was quite difficult. Deep inside I sensed what it was, but the guilt and shame often consumed and left me fearful and apprehensive about speaking it out loud. Then again, I trusted Joe and felt safe with him. I also knew from past experiences that when in a challenging emotional situation giving voice to my feelings helped bring them to the surface so they could be released. This had often led me to then feeling more peaceful and at ease.

My voice was shaking as I said, "I want my freedom, Joe. I want more time with John and to be able to do more things together. I also want to be with my friends. I'd love to go on some retreats for myself. But I can't do these things because of the care Gidget requires. I am only able to be gone for about five hours because I have to get back home to express her bladder. Even then, there is often a mess to clean up when I return.

"And—it's hard for me to say this as it feels incredibly selfish—but what about my quality of life? Whenever I think about it, I feel resentful, followed by guilt because I genuinely do love Gidget. She can't help it that she has IVDD and can't control her bladder. I also was well aware of all of this when I adopted her. But there are days where I feel at the end of my rope and just can't cope. In all honesty, I sense there will be some relief when I won't have to care for her anymore."

After everything had spilled out, I felt some relief in sharing openly what was on my heart, though the guilt and shame remained. I couldn't shake the feeling that I was a terrible person for having these feelings, and it was overwhelming.

Joe assured me everything I was feeling was natural, and I sensed no judgment from him. This was a pressure I was putting on myself, though I didn't know how to stop.

"I have two questions I'd like you to think about," he said.

"Okay."

"First, can you be okay with owning and feeling all of your emotions?"

This should be doable, I thought, but a part of me was just so drained. I didn't want to feel all the feelings anymore. But I said, "I'm willing to keep working on that."

"I'm glad to hear this. It's really important that you feel all your feelings. Especially the ones that feel most uncomfortable."

Trying to reassure myself, I said, "I can do this."

"Second, can you be okay with not knowing right now?"

While I understood this as meaning the question of whether or not I should euthanize Gidget, it felt incredibly difficult.

My whole body was in a knot. I was also holding my breath, while my throat was constricted and felt as if it was on fire. I honestly didn't know if I could be okay with not knowing. I wanted to know *now* what the right thing was to do.

For what felt like forever a silence hung between us. Finally, in barely a whisper that took everything within me, I said, "I'll try."

"I know it's not easy, but I also believe you can do this."

I couldn't speak, nodding my head up and down, while tears wanted to explode to the surface. But I held them in.

We agreed to talk again the following week.

"Thanks so much, Joe," I said. "I don't know how to thank you for being here for me."

After our call ended, I sat and stared out the window with tears streaming down my face. Nothing was clear yet, but some of the intense internal pressure I'd felt had lightened its grip on me.

I don't know how long I sat in my writing cottage, just looking out the window, but I realized I was tired and in need of a nap. I wanted to be rested when John got home from work.

John knew I had spoken with Joe that morning, and he fully supported my reaching out for help. That evening, we sat in the living room as we often do to share what our days were like and I found I felt calm and relaxed as I told him about the conversation. It would, however, lead to something I didn't expect.

I said, "I recall a time before Frankie passed away when I tried to prepare you for the fact I'd want another special needs dachshund to care for once she was gone. I sensed your hesitancy about it, but it was something I felt strongly called to do. I simply couldn't imagine my life without another one to care for.

"Now," I continued, "I find myself thinking that perhaps it's time to move on from caring for a special needs dog, even though I'm struggling internally with the many feelings I'm having."

John nodded in agreement.

"There have been plenty of times over the years when I've felt guilty for having a disabled dog because of the limits it placed on plans we wanted to make, along with the financial burden."

John said, "Knowing we had restrictions because of Frankie and Joie, and now Gidget… it's why I just go to work."

Usually a statement like that would have caused me to feel shame and guilt, and I would have angrily defended myself. I felt none of this now. I realized that just as I was sharing my feelings honestly, so was John. It had never crossed my mind what he did to cope, but I appreciated that he felt comfortable telling me.

"That's interesting. I feel in one way I wanted pets because you work so much."

John takes great pride in his work, as I do, and we both have a tendency at times to lose ourselves in it and then neglect other aspects of life. We do, however, try to remind each other of this when one of us feels out of balance or unfulfilled.

"I don't know yet what the right and best situation is regarding Gidget, but I do know that someday when she's gone, I want to spend more time with you. I'd also like to experience just being able to get up and go when we want and go places we've talked about. I do believe that Gidget will be the last disabled dog I'll adopt and care for."

John softly said, "I'm glad to hear you say this. It hasn't always been easy."

"I know." Tears welled in my eyes as I felt some regret for what John may have sacrificed.

"But I did love them and learned from them, too," he added.

"I'm happy to hear that. I feel the same way."

Like any marriage, ours has had many ups and downs, twists and turns, and I'm grateful for how far John and I have come in communicating with each other. I reflected on the months leading to our wedding all those years ago, when we went through a series of counseling sessions which were required by the minister in order for him to marry us.

The minister had seemed to know John well, and in his opinion it wasn't always easy for John to share what he was feeling, and how he needed time to process his emotions first. I, on the other hand, wanted to speak right away about what was on my mind.

Though I thought I understood and accepted the minister's observations, it would take me quite a few years to be okay with how John processed his feelings and challenges. There were times I just *knew* something was on his mind, though he'd often deny it. I'd have to practice patience and just wait it out. I'd come to realize that most times my hunch was correct, and while we laugh about this today, there were times it drove me crazy! I've no doubt at times too that my insisting I know at the moment what was bugging him drove him crazy too.

Over the years we have balanced out nicely. I have learned to respect John's need to contemplate, and that inward contemplation is vital for me as well. John has learned he can trust me with his feelings, even those that feel uncomfortable. And I learned to trust myself and my own feelings more.

CHAPTER 24

Pet Caregiver Burden

AFTER THE WEEKEND and the beautiful and honest discussion John and I had engaged in, I continued to work on being okay with "not knowing." I also did more research on the internet. I just didn't believe I was the only one who struggled with the tug and pull I was feeling.

I eventually came across an article by Melissa Dahl titled, *I Spent Thousands to Keep My Sick Cat Alive. I Don't Think I'd Do It Again.*

Melissa's ten-year-old cat had been diagnosed with a terminal heart condition. It would be nearly two-and-half years later when the cat died in what Melissa described as, "a cold and unfamiliar emergency room in the middle of the night."

She wrote:

> *"This was a longer prognosis than any vet predicted, and yet, in the months since her death, I can't stop wondering whether I did the right thing in delaying the inevitable for so long. The twice-a-day pills, the bi-monthly visits to the veterinary cardiologist (which almost always included a chest tap, a risky, invasive procedure that drained fluid from in and around her lungs), not to mention the vast sums of money spent on it all: Were these things really for her, or were they mostly, selfishly, for*

me? Saying goodbye to a pet has never been easy, but advances in modern veterinary care can make it near-impossible for pet owners to know when to let go. It's an ethical quandary that's in some ways unsettlingly similar to aging and end-of-life issues currently plaguing human medicine. Just because we can extend life, should we?"

After reading the article I reflected on a memory early on in my marriage when we brought home a chocolate Lab puppy. I had talked about wanting a puppy for two years before John finally agreed. At that point I was working close to home and could easily check on the growing pup during my lunch hour. That dog was Cassie Jo.

I recalled as she grew older how I'd often think about what I'd do if she were diagnosed with a life-threatening disease. I'd do anything I could to help her. I'd sell my car and whatever possessions I could to pay for whatever she needed. Unfortunately, my devotion would be put to the test when in her ninth year of life she was diagnosed with terminal bone cancer.

Without treatment the vet said she would likely only live another two to three months. Even though chemotherapy and radiation were considered, they weren't viable options. The tumor, which had begun to grow on her hip, was also touching her spine making surgery too risky. We finally decided on an experimental drug, which was administered once a month. Early studies showed promise in slowing the progression of the growth of the tumor, and in Cassie Jo's case it did exactly that. She lived another ten months of quality life.

As I reflected on this, my thoughts turned to the mix of emotions I was feeling regarding Gidget and her health. Though she didn't have a terminal illness, her chronic issues required her to be subjected to endless rounds of medication, prodding and poking. Once again I asked myself, truly, when was enough, enough?

I also came across an article from Time.com titled, *People with Sick Pets Have More Anxiety and Depression.* I certainly resonated with feeling anxious, though I didn't feel I was depressed.

In part, the article stated:

> "More than 90% of pet owners think of their dog or cat as a member of their family, according to a 2015 Harris Poll. While that close bond

makes pets a boon to human happiness—and even, in many cases, to mental health—it can also come with a downside. New research suggests that when people care for ill pets, they have more depression, anxiety and caregiving distress: symptoms that are similar to how people report feeling when caring for sick relatives, the study authors say."

Gidget wasn't sick per se, but she did have recurring bladder infections, along with taking medication to manage her seizures. Also, the extra care taking of a special needs pet that can't urinate on their own certainly had me feeling more stressed.

It was then I came across a first of its kind study published in the Veterinary Record journal. The study was implemented by Mary Beth Spitznagel, Ph.D., who specializes in neuropsychology—the study of the relationship between behavior, emotion and cognition and brain function.

Dr. Spitznagel began her research on caregiver burden in family members of people with dementia. It was only after her dog was diagnosed with transitional cell carcinoma, Cushing's disease, and cognitive dementia that she decided to expand her research on caregiver burden and it effects to pet owners.

For the research, Dr. Spitznagel conducted a survey of two hundred thirty-eight owners of dogs and cats. Half the animals had a chronic or terminal illness and the other half were healthy. Those who took part in the survey completed questions asking about how taking care of a pet affected them.

As I read Spitnagel's findings I felt like they were describing me. People caring for sick pets definitely experienced caregiver burden—including its trademark feelings of anxiety, stress, and depression, along with a lower quality of life—as those who tended to their chronically ill human relatives.

What really surprised me, though, was that most of the 248 participants of the study—98%, in fact—were female. They were also an average of 48 years old, highly educated, and of a fairly high socioeconomic class. Though more research is needed about how different groups of people interact with their pets, the researchers felt this group was the most likely to choose to keep an animal with a terminal illness or chronic disease alive despite the financial costs or emotional effects.

Knowing I wasn't alone, and that what I had been feeling was not only real but had a name, helped to lift some of my burden. I wanted to know more and went to their website, Petcaregiverburden.com.

This organization is dedicated to the science of caregiver burden in the pet owner, and the understanding of how the owner's experience impacts others, including the veterinarian and the pet. The articles on their site are quite impactful, though there was one in particular that resonated for me—*Am I a Burdened Caregiver?*

The first two sentences—"I love my pet. Why am I so stressed out?"—really tugged at my heart. As I've shared to this point, I was constantly engaged in a battle with myself, torn between my love for Gidget and my feeling like I'd lost all coping abilities, which also caused me to feel resentment and anger. When I read the following paragraph it really hit home:

> *"A burdened caregiver may feel angry or strained when they are around their loved one, but part of the anger may actually come from fear or uncertainty. For example, a caregiver may feel afraid of the future, or uncertain about what treatment choices to make. Experiences of guilt are also common—the caregiver may believe s/he should be doing a better job, or doing more to provide care."*

The article resonated on so many levels and had me breathing a sigh of relief. From how psychological distress is common, to being affected on a physical level, to looking at financial strain, and how one's quality of life can feel diminished, it was everything I was experiencing.

The conclusion was that while taking care of a terminal or sick pet has many rewards, it is easy to give until it hurts, thus leading to feelings of overwhelm and despair. It's important when one feels this way to ask for help and to recognize that this does not mean they are weak or uncaring. The article also mentioned how vital it is to look closely at all the issues at play, consider how they affect your life, and what you may be able to do to manage or improve things.

I had certainly tried to do this on my own and had continued to feel like I was drowning. It was in finding out there were others out there who understood and could offer guidance that I felt the first glimmer of hope return.

CHAPTER 25

Not Alone

THE RESEARCH ON pet caregiver burden impacted me so much that I emailed the founder, Mary Beth, to express my gratitude for her study. I also told her that I was experiencing much of what her study participants had and that if it would be helpful I would be happy to participate in any further studies she may conduct.

In the meantime, daily life went on, which for me meant balancing Gidget's needs with my work and running our home. I expressed Gidget's bladder every few hours, yet there were many days when she still had accidents and I would have to stop whatever else I was doing to clean up. In quieter times this was merely frustrating; on days when I had many projects and errands on my plate, I'd feel stretched to my limit. I'd question what I was doing wrong or what more I should be doing, or perhaps did I need to be more attentive to her?

To make matters worse, the frequency of her overnight accidents was increasing. It was not uncommon for Gidget to have an accident one or two nights in a week, but now more and more I was waking to find her bed soaked in urine and her sitting in her own feces. Those days began not only with cleaning up a mess, but worrying that this would lead to yet another bladder infection.

Each time her collected urine was sent to the lab to find out what was causing the infection, the result was E. coli. This meant the bacteria from the feces had entered her vulva. It left me feeling like I was fighting a losing battle.

Her infections were back-to-back that winter and I was once again nearing the end of my rope. It had me questioning so many things I'd not considered before as I tried to grasp what the "right" thing was to do. I recalled thinking how unfair it was to let her sit in her own "shit and stink." I certainly wouldn't want that for myself.

I also read more about Mary Beth's survey and was once again struck by the fact that the vast majority of participants were female. More importantly, though, I appreciated how the researchers pointed out that those caregiving for four-legged family members endured the same rollercoaster ride of overwhelm, guilt, fear and resentment as those caring for a sick human. As there were already a plethora of studies on human-to-human caregiving, these similarities could help researchers identify how they could help pet caregivers reduce their burdensome feelings.

Interestingly, the study did not look at the participants' lives leading up to the point the pet became sick. That meant they couldn't know for sure the root causes of the anxiety and depression these women expressed and whether they were directly related to the burden of caregiving or a culmination of things. For me, this would prove to be a key factor in discovering the root cause.

The researchers also pointed out that the selection of participants may have been somewhat slanted, as some with an ill pet will choose euthanasia rather than long-term care. Therefore, those who participated in the study may have an especially close bond to their pets.

Caring for an ill pet can be stressful for anyone; however, the researchers also acknowledged that while some who make the choice to care for an ill pet experience a normal amount of stress, others find themselves unable to cope. Having lived through both sides of the coin, this deeply resonated with me.

The articles provided by Mary Beth and her team were definitely beneficial to me, but they brought me no closer to figuring out what the best path was for me and Gidget. I found myself wishing the study was further along and provided resources.

In the meantime I tried to lean into the support system I did have, including my women's mastermind circle, which met each month at one of our homes. It was always a treat to meet at Pam's place out in the country, especially when the weather was nice and we could sit in the tepee. It was her turn that April, but as it was a cold and windy day we met in the cozy lower level of her home.

When it came to my turn to talk I took a deep breath. Everyone knew I was struggling with the challenges around caring for Gidget, as I'd expressed this in February when I hosted our group, then again at our meeting in March. It was no surprise to them when I brought the subject up again.

I told them that there had been some hopeful developments since the last time I saw them, including the research I'd come across and the talk I had with Joe, as well as my discussion with John. Yet, despite all of this I still didn't know what to do. When I was done sharing, Lisa and Monica offered their input. They both said pretty much the same thing—when the time was right, should I choose to euthanize Gidget, I would know.

It was the same advice I'd personally given to many others over the years, but it didn't feel true for me. As the room grew quiet, I hugged the large pillow on my lap and stared into space.

A few moments later, Pam broke the silence. "Can I ask you something, Barb?"

I nodded my head up and down.

With the deepest of compassion in her voice, she said, "What do you really want?"

The moment she said this I felt a ball of fire rise up from the lower part of belly. It traveled through my chest and into my throat, where it got stuck. It felt like my throat was burning. As I held tight to the pillow, I somehow mustered the courage to finally say, "I want to let her go!"

These words seemed to come from somewhere deep within, and once they escaped my lips I put the pillow to my face and sank into the corner of the sofa as if trying to make myself small. I felt so much shame and guilt it was as if I was being swallowed whole. The room was once again silent.

It felt like an eternity, but I eventually dropped the pillow away from my face. As I looked around the room, looking into each one of their faces, I could feel their support and love for me. While they understood that this was a decision I had to make on my own and that there was no easy answer, they'd held this sacred space of honoring of what it was I needed to express.

As I drove home after our gathering, I felt numb. I knew I needed to be with what had transpired even though I wasn't sure how to exactly do that.

The following Tuesday I talked with Joe again. I shared with him the conversation I'd had with John. I said it opened up a new understanding between us. John supported me on whatever decision I made regarding Gidget, but it was still up to me to actually make the decision.

I also told him what happened during my women's circle and the lingering guilt and shame over what I had expressed, as well as my discovery of the Pet Caregiver Burden website and their study. It helped, I said, to know I wasn't alone in the feelings I was experiencing.

When I had finished, Joe asked, "How is Gidget doing?"

"She just completed her last round of antibiotics, so I don't know yet if the infection is completely gone. Time will tell. She is still having accidents overnight. In all honesty, this still causes me to feel stressed, and keeps me in this loop of questioning whether I'm doing what is best for her."

I paused for a moment before continuing.

"I just don't know, Joe. Can I continue like this? Is this a quality of life for Gidget? And as difficult as this still is to say, what about my quality of life? I feel so torn."

Joe reminded me of my support team, emphasizing how fortunate I was to have my mom, John, my women's circle, my best friend Victoria, and of course, Dawn, to talk with.

"And you," I said.

"Yes, you can call me anytime."

"I know, and I'm grateful for that. Thank you."

I agreed to continue to be in the question of not knowing and scheduled another time to talk with Joe the following week.

Those conversations with Joe and the others I confided in brought me hope and comfort in a dark time. Yet this support, I realized, wasn't the complete solution. The fact remained that I didn't want to "sit with not knowing"; I wanted to resolve how I was feeling *now*. I wanted the suffering to end. It was excruciating, and it felt like it was increasing rather than subsiding.

CHAPTER 26

The Choice

THE MORNING FOLLOWING my talk with Joe I awoke to find Gidget sitting in an explosion of feces and her bed completely soaked with urine. I started to cry. Trying to maneuver her carefully out of her kennel and not drag her further through the mess, some of the poop fell onto the floor, while at the same time she leaked more urine. I quickly scrambled to get her to the bathroom.

Holding her over the toilet and expressing what little was still left in her, I cried, "Gidget, I just don't know what to do!"

I grabbed a bath towel and whisked her off to the kitchen sink to wash her down. As I soaped her little body, my mind continued to spin. I felt like this was never going to end.

Once she was clean, I towel dried her, then put on her fleece coat to keep her warm until she was completely dry.

My emotions were a roller coaster. One moment I was so frustrated and then I'd look at Gidget's sweet face and feel bad she had to deal yet again with my negative energy. She couldn't help what was happening with her body. I'd then hug her close to my chest, cuddling her and assuring her I loved her.

After she was clean, I prepared her breakfast with her dose of potassium bromide, three herbs and a bladder supplement sprinkled on top, plus a splash of water. My mind continued to whirl, thinking how I wouldn't want to eat my food with all this crap piled on top. *Was this really fair to Gidget?*

Here I was again drowning in a sea of unknowns. I was numb. I couldn't get the image of what I had woken to—Gidget sitting in that dirty kennel yet again—out of my mind.

I felt like crawling back into bed and hiding away from all my angst, wishing it would just all magically disappear, but I had a haircut scheduled mid-morning.

As I walked out to my writing cottage, it took every ounce of energy to put one front in front of the other. I had intended to do some work before my hair appointment, but instead I plopped onto my wicker chair and cried.

I thought about what the vet had said to me about the choices pet owners have when their pets have chronic health issues, and when their quality of life is declining. But then I heard Dawn telling me that the first thing she'd heard from Gidget was that she was fine just the way she was. Round and round these two competing images went through my mind.

I also continued to struggle with the true meaning of Gidget's message— was she "fine" if I let her go? Or "okay" having chronic bladder infections? Fine with constant UTIs and having to have a needle injected into her bladder? Okay sitting in her feces and urine? Though it seemed impossible that she was content living this way, there was simply no way I could know for sure.

One thing I did know was that it was only eight a.m. and already I was in a state of agony and feeling like I was going to burst at any moment.

Maybe some time at the salon would help, I thought as I drove to my appointment. I always looked forward to having my hair washed and my scalp massaged, and the conversations I had with Missy, the compassionate and sweet woman who did my hair. Hairdressers have a reputation for being good listeners as well as stylists, and this was definitely the case with Missy. Over the years we had talked about a wide variety of issues and challenges, as well as the celebrated victories in our lives, and I had come to think of her as a dear friend.

As I climbed into her chair, however, I was so thoroughly drained I wasn't sure I wanted to talk about what I was going through. I don't know if Missy picked up on my energy, but her genuine caring drew me out and I soon found myself opening up to her. Missy understood that there was no right answer, and that I had to make this decision on my own, but I was thankful for the empathy I felt from her.

Later, as I stood at the counter to pay for the haircut, Missy and the salon owner were chatting about something. I don't even recall what they were saying because all I could think was that it all seemed so unimportant. I felt as though I was stuck in a fog that just wouldn't clear.

A familiar feeling of anxiousness rose to the surface as I grew more impatient with their conversation. They were trying to engage me but I was desperately trying to find a polite way to make my exit. Finally, I said I really had to go, then gave Missy a hug and quickly made my way out to my car.

It was on the drive back home that I knew I couldn't live like this anymore. I had made my decision. I was going to let Gidget go.

The minute I walked through the door and took my coat off I dialed Joe's number. I got his voice mail. My voice shook as tears rolled down my face. I left him a message telling him of my choice and said I felt it was the right thing to do. I also asked him to please call me when he had a chance.

After I left the message, my body was trembling. I then called John who was on a job site and let him know my decision.

"Okay, honey," he said softly, "Let me know if you need me."

Trying to show him I was strong, I said, "I'll be okay. I'm going to call the vet office once I hang up with you."

My voice caught in my throat before I could continue. "I'm also going to ask Dr. Mary if she can come to the house to euthanize Gidget. I'm hoping she can come on Friday as I'd like one more day with Gidget."

"Okay."

After we said we loved each other and hung up, I dialed the vet clinic. The receptionist on the other end of the line had always loved it when I brought Gidget in.

Crying I said, "I need to make an appointment to put Gidget to sleep. It's time."

I could hear the compassion in her voice as she said, "Oh, I'm so sorry to hear this."

"I know. Me too," I said. "But I'd first like to talk to Dr. Mary. If she could please call me when she has a moment, I'd appreciate it. I'd really like her to come to my house to put Gidget to sleep, if possible."

"Well, why don't we schedule the appointment and I'll have Dr. Mary call you when she gets in this afternoon."

"Okay. Well, I really want one more day with Gidget so I'd like to schedule it for Friday."

Dr. Mary wasn't in the office on Thursdays so I was able to schedule the appointment for her to come to my house mid-morning on Friday. I also requested the vet technician I felt most comfortable with. I was relieved she worked on Friday and could accompany Dr. Mary.

As soon as I hung up the phone, I called my mom to let her know of my decision. The minute I heard her voice my throat tightened. I tried to control the tears as I choked out those terrible words. It felt like a blur. But the one thing I remember vividly was saying that I just didn't feel it was fair that Gidget had to keep sitting in her own 'shit and stink.' Little did I know this would actually turn out to be a message for me.

It was around one o'clock when Dr. Mary called. Thinking back on that conversation, I realize I still had doubts that I was doing the right thing. But I couldn't see it. All I could feel was the pain I was in.

I remember saying, "If I change my mind can I call you?"

"Of course," she said. "Even if it's last minute, don't hesitate to call the office."

After I hung up, I continued to sit on the ottoman in my writing cottage, where I'd gone when Dr. Mary called. Again, I felt that awfulness seeping through every part of me. This feeling had been plaguing me the past few months and it wasn't letting up.

It was mid-afternoon when I heard back from Joe. I reiterated my decision and the reason why, then told him the appointment was for Friday. I'd be taking the next day to spend quality time with Gidget and say my goodbyes.

He said, "I see. Will you promise to call me this weekend or next week? You've taken me on this journey and I'd really like to know how you are doing."

"Of course," I said. "I promise I will do that when I feel up to it."

I had just set my phone down on my desk when I heard a ping on my computer notifying me of a new email. It was from Dawn.

She had written to let me know how much she was enjoying *Expedition Happiness,* the documentary I had told her about. It's about two young kids, free spirits really, and their dog Rudi, who travel in a bus they converted into a home on wheels, in search of something more. They ultimately return home when Rudi becomes sick.

After reading Dawn's email, I realized I had to share my decision with her, as she too had walked this journey with Gidget and me. Little did I know that what was about to transpire would bring me to my knees.

CHAPTER 27

Surrendering

IT WASN'T A coincidence that Dawn's email came through right after I hung up with Joe. Though I still believed we are sent signs from the Universe to guide us, that doesn't mean it will always be smooth sailing. Remembering that Spirit has our back and our best interest in mind can also be difficult, especially when we feel in the depths of wanting to run from something that is causing us a great deal of pain.

I immediately wrote back to Dawn to let her know I'd made a decision for Gidget. I don't recall whether she asked to chat via video conference or I did. Whatever the case, a short time later we were face-to-face via our computer screens.

As an animal communicator for a good part of her life and one who can read energy, Dawn shared with me her honest thoughts encouraging me to rethink my decision. Later, I would come to realize how difficult this was for her. She was walking a delicate line, and she knew it, but her duty as my friend took precedence over any trepidation she might have felt.

At the time, however, I strongly rebelled against what she was saying. I couldn't see that by holding space and sharing with me honestly, she really did want what was best for all involved. All I felt was judgment and tried to defend myself accordingly.

As we went back and forth, the inner pressure I felt was escalating. I became more and more upset. I felt like I wasn't being supported for my decision. I vividly recall at one point yelling, "You have no idea what my life is like!"

It's true that we can never truly know what another's life is like unless we've walked in their shoes. But the fact was that Dawn and I had been friends for five years and had a strong connection. This was evidenced by the fact that I had chosen her with whom to express the pain I'd carried of being touched inappropriately as a child, something I had never shared with anyone before that.

The more we talked, the more agitated and uncomfortable I became. Finally, Dawn said, "I'm not sure what else I can do to help you, Barb."

I know now she was also struggling with how best to help me, but all I felt was that she just didn't understand what I was going through.

I also wanted more than anything for her to say she trusted my decision. We reached a crossroads in our conversation when she said, "I'm just trying to be an advocate for Gidget."

A rage inside me rushed to the surface. Clenching my right hand into a fist, I punched it into my left hand. With a knot in my throat and my voice cracking, I yelled, "But who was an advocate for me?"

I was taken aback by the outburst that came tumbling out my mouth, along with this now familiar mix of guilt and shame that had plagued me. But I also felt oddly relieved.

I don't recall how we ended the conversation. All I felt was I had nothing left in me and I was still trying to make sense of it all. But I remembered that Dawn encouraged me to be with my feelings and to spend time with Gidget.

I recall saying I would, but I also remember wondering what good it would do. By now it was late afternoon and I felt absolutely drained of all energy.

I walked back into the house, made my way to the sofa and plopped myself down. Within moments Gidget was sitting on the floor looking up at me. I felt some resistance about picking her up, but I also knew my time with her was limited. I didn't want her last hours with me to be like this.

As Gidget's long body snuggled alongside me and her head rested in the crook of my arm, her eyes looking at me, tears rose to the surface once again and trickled down the side of my face. I was so tired of crying.

My body felt like a ton of cement was weighing it down. I thought I might possibly never be able to move again. I was mentally exhausted. I just didn't want to think anymore. I wondered, *what was there really to give thought to anymore?*

When John arrived home a half-hour later I was still lying on the couch with Gidget. I could barely muster a hello to him. He knew I'd made the decision to put Gidget to sleep, but he wasn't aware of the conversation I'd just had with Dawn.

He went into his office to do some paperwork. A few minutes after five he walked back into the living room to find I'd not moved from the sofa. It was a Wednesday night, our "date night," when we typically went out to eat somewhere. Usually at this time I'd be in the bedroom freshening up my makeup and changing my clothes. But I couldn't move from the couch.

John said, "Aren't we going out for date night?"

I shook my head no.

As John walked away, I could see the disappointment on his face. This only caused me to feel more guilt. For a brief moment, I thought I should just power through and force myself to go even though I just couldn't imagine how I was going to.

Instead, I remember telling myself I just had to sit with the uncomfortableness of disappointing him. Once again this caused tears to roll down my cheeks. Why did I feel like all I was doing was disappointing others?

So many thoughts ran through my mind. *Why couldn't I get it together? Why does this all have to be so hard? Why does everything have to be so painful?*

Then a thought ran across my mind that startled me. I heard, *I'd rather die than deal with this pain.* It shook me to my core, so much so that I actually wondered who had just said it. It couldn't have been me. In all my fifty-four years, I didn't recall ever feeling like I'd rather die than face something, no matter how painful.

The truth was that *it was me*—but there was also a part of me that didn't want to die. In that moment, realized I could continue to live in fear of this emotional pain that was trying to swallow me whole, or I could choose to find a way to love myself through this excruciating time.

It was around eight o'clock when I made my way to bed. I still didn't know how I was going to move through the pain, but this new awareness that I had a choice was a step in the right direction.

I found John already asleep, which was another wakeup call. We'd be going to sleep without saying goodnight. I turned the light off on my nightstand but I was wide awake. As I lay there, I thought about all the times I had prayed for guidance for myself or asked for blessings for someone I know is in need. Many times I had begged for answers, but tonight was different.

I'd heard of others surrendering when in the depths of despair, but it wasn't until this moment that I felt like I understood what that meant. It was the only thing I could do now. I had to trust.

I wasn't sure how this was going to unfold. But then I realized I could either hold tightly to these reins of control, or I could have faith that if I completely surrendered that I indeed would be guided.

And so I did just that. I didn't beg. I didn't try bargaining. I just surrendered to a higher power, asking that I be shown what it was I needed to do next. I couldn't do this alone anymore.

Around two a.m. I awoke and knew what had to be done. I was still scared, but I also trusted it would be okay and I drifted back to sleep.

When I awoke again at six a.m., a heaviness still plagued me. I wasn't sure what was helping me to put one foot in front of the other. But I also knew what I had to do even though I wasn't sure exactly how I would do it. All I knew was that it had to be *today*. I couldn't wait any longer.

I walked into the kitchen and saw John at the counter packing his lunch for work. I scooped Gidget into my arms, sat down at the kitchen table, and placed her on my lap. John looked over at me asking how I was.

"I need to talk to you."

"Okay, but I need to be across the street to meet sub-contractors in twenty minutes."

"This is really important."

"What's up?"

I hadn't planned how I was going to say anything, I just trusted I was being guided.

"How does Gidget look to you?"

As he stood off to the side, he looked at her, then me, and said, "She looks sick."

I shook my head back and forth as I summoned the courage to say what I knew needed to be said.

After a moment I quietly said, "She's not sick, John."

"She's not?"

"No. It's me. I'm sick."

"What do you mean?"

"I need to tell you something that has caused me a great deal of pain for many years, but I've been so afraid to tell you."

As he knelt beside me, he put his hand on my shoulder. "It's okay, you can tell me."

With every ounce of courage I could muster, I took a deep breath and wailed out that I'd been inappropriately touched as a child, this secret, I'd been carrying with me for far too long.

I had no idea how he would react. I was terrified he wouldn't understand and that he may even leave me, thinking I was damaged. My whole body was shaking.

He put his arms around me as I continued to cry and said, "It's going to be okay. We will get through this."

It was such a relief to hear him say this.

After a few moments, he stood up and said, "You need to trust God to help you."

A half-smile came across my face. "I did. That's why I just shared this with you."

"You know I'm here for you, right?"

I nodded my head up and down. We've had our ups and downs, but we've always been there for each other. Over the years we have often fondly referred to ourselves as Team Techel.

"But I also trust that whatever you need to do for support you will find a way. I know you've been searching for a long time. This has been what it's been all about, hasn't it?"

I nodded again and said, "I know. A big part of my healing has come just by sharing the pain of what happened to me with you after keeping it locked inside for all these years. I have Dawn and Joe to thank for helping me finally reach this point."

I patted Gidget on the head and added, "And oh my gosh, I can't forget Gidget. She was truly instrumental in helping me."

"I love you, honey. We will get through this. We always do."

"I know," I said.

"I really do need to get to work. Are you going to be okay?"

"I'm fine, really. I'm also going to talk to my mom today if she's home."

"Oh good, I'm glad to hear that."

I stood with Gidget still in my arms and we had a group hug. As John turned toward the door he looked back, and with tears in his eyes he said, "Thank you for helping Mama, Gidget."

At that moment I didn't think I could love this man any more than I already did.

CHAPTER 28

Getting Help

I CONTINUED TO follow Spirit's guidance and sent a text to my mom asking if she was home and could I come over.

Within moments I received her text: yes.

I've never given birth to a child so I could only imagine how this is when you get a call, text, or email from one of your children saying they need to talk. Oh, moms have to be so strong! This has definitely been my mom. Not a day goes by that I don't feel deep gratitude for our relationship. There's pretty much nothing I can't share with her, yet for years just the thought of telling her what had happened to me as a child had conjured up feelings of anxiety and fear.

Today, however, I was at peace as I made the short ten-minute drive to her house. It wasn't going to be easy. I knew the news would cause Mom to go through her own anguish, but I trusted Spirit would guide her just as I'd been guided to this point.

Before I knew it I was greeting her at the door, then, finally, telling her of the excruciating event that had haunted me for decades. When I was finished, there was no judgment, just the fear and self-doubt I'd held onto for so long melting away in the loving arms of my mom.

There were tears, of course, on both our parts. Mom said she wished she had known and would have done everything in her power to prevent further damage, and I told her that as a young child I was unable to put into words what had happened. I also explained that I had buried the memory so deeply that it didn't surface into my consciousness until I was twenty-nine years old. Most importantly, I made it clear that it wasn't her fault.

That conversation, while draining, left me feeling freer than ever I had in my life. My body no longer felt weighted down by a ton of bricks. I also had a sense of calm I had never experienced before. The mental anguish I'd been struggling with had dissipated immensely.

As I moved through the next few days and spoke with Joe and Dawn, there were moments it all felt quite surreal. I had moments of panic and the thought *Did that just really happen?* would run through my mind.

The feelings were so intense that a part of me wanted to take back what I had expressed. But I would learn this was normal as I grew into this new space. Integrating the experience entirely into my being would take time and was not to be rushed.

As the days and weeks unfolded, I realized I'd convinced myself that the answer to my resentment, anger, and pain was to let Gidget go. I still felt some guilt for that. But I also knew this time of integration was learning about not beating myself up for what *might* have been. This wouldn't serve Gidget, me, or anyone any good.

I now had an opportunity to begin again. It was up to me to keep working with, and moving into, this newly expanded space I had opened within me. The support I'd received from Joe and Dawn had helped get me to this point and I trusted I would be guided to the next steps I needed to embrace.

I also began to recognize the many signs I had received in the past that I had more healing do around my childhood. One thing that came to mind was a therapy session I had back in the fall of 2017, six months before I told my mom and John what had happened to me as a child. The therapist used EMDR® (Eye Movement Desensitization and Reprocessing), a technique that can help in releasing and reprocessing traumatic memories. It has also been shown to help reduce anxiety and stress surrounding almost any life struggle or negative event, and to shift negative beliefs into more positive ones.

As we moved deeper into EMDR, there came a point where I experienced what felt like a heavy cloak of darkness that started at my shoulders and slowly moved down my entire body. I would learn from the therapist that this was unresolved grief from the childhood wound, that I had never grieved for that lost part of myself. It seemed so clear after the session, but it also left me astounded that it never occurred to me that I needed to fully experience the sorrow.

To further support my healing I scheduled a massage, which I knew could help release built-up toxins in the body caused by stress or emotional pain. I also found, in the course of my research, the work of Dr. Judith Kravitz and the technique she developed called Transformational Breath®. Breathwork can also help release various emotions experienced through trauma or life challenges.

There wasn't anyone in my immediate area that offered this healing modality, but I soon found two practitioners in two larger cities near me. Reading the bios and websites of both women, I followed my intuition as to which one I felt comfortable with, then booked a session for the week after my massage.

Before my breathwork appointment I watched a video about the breathing technique. It caused me to feel a little nervous. The method, as described on the website, "utilizes a full relaxed breath that originates in the lower abdomen and repeats the inhalation and exhalation without pausing."

I've had asthma since I was three years old and worried I wouldn't have the lung capacity to do this type of breathing. So often in my life, I've felt like a fish out of water, gasping for air! But at the same time, I trusted it would be beneficial. I reminded myself that I was also going to someone who was trained and skilled in this technique and would be guiding me through the process.

Over the years I'd come to believe and appreciate the connection between mind, body, and spirit. I revisited Dr. Judith Kravitz' website once again before my appointment and I was comforted to learn that this type of modality has shown to also help with spiritual awareness, strengthening the connection with the Divine, and expanding awareness.

I had always believed in the conceptual aspect of God, but I had been struggling for as long as I could remember to understand what God really was in my life. The dogma of a judgmental God and one sometimes depicted as a white man with a white beard in the sky just didn't work for me.

But if that wasn't God, who was He/She? Could we even label God as female or male? A part of me has always felt more comfortable with expressing God as Spirit or the Divine—an energy so vast and significant that we can't truly comprehend it. For the most part I trusted It is real and is guiding me, though I sometimes had my doubts.

The day arrived for my two-hour breathwork session with Parnee. After an hour-long drive, I arrived at an old industrial complex. Parnee was located at the back of the lot. I had some apprehension as I walked through the door as the space was large, cold, and open. But Parnee greeted me with a warm welcome, then invited me to follow her to another room, a small, quaint space lit only by two small salt lamps. Parnee motioned for me to take a seat right inside the door.

After asking what had brought me to her, she explained the pattern of the breathwork she'd be coaching me through during our time together.

It would begin with an inhalation that starts at the lower abdomen to then bringing the breath up through the diaphragm and out the mouth in exhalation. All of these breaths are done without pausing and continue for an extended period, and with the mouth open the entire time.

She would guide me on how long I had to keep the breathing pattern going and let me know when to stop. She would then instruct me to pound my legs, arms, and hands, almost as if throwing a tantrum. Again, she'd coach me through when to start and when to stop, and then return to the breathing pattern.

As I climbed onto the massage table and lay on my back, Parnee placed a bolster under my knees. She then asked me to breathe normally so could witness my breathing pattern.

I wasn't really surprised when she commented that my breathing was quite shallow. Though this is the case for many, I had often wondered if mine was more so because of the asthma.

Before the session began, Parnee said she would also be applying pressure points to certain parts of my upper body to release any energy that was stuck.

Lastly, Parnee said I could set an intention for the session, though it wasn't necessary if I didn't have one. The breathwork would do what it needed to. I chose to focus on finding more peace and healing, not only for what Gidget and I had just been through, but also for anything from my past that had held me back to this point.

"Do you have any questions before we begin?" Parnee asked.

"I'm a little nervous about my mouth becoming dry during the session. I have a dry mouth to begin with."

"This is common, but only temporary. Try not to worry about it."

"Okay."

As the session began and we moved through the breathwork, I had to continually remind myself not to panic about my mouth feeling dry. I'd repeat silently to myself, *just stay in the present moment.* The breathing wasn't easy, but it wasn't hard either. It was just different.

I did feel lightheaded, which was normal according to the website. It said that the first few times you practice this type of breathing you can experience symptoms of hyperventilation. I reminded myself I was under the care of someone who knew what they were doing and to relax and be open to the experience.

I don't recall all the different areas she applied pressure on my body except for two. The first was an area on the right side of my neck, a few inches under my ear.

"Ouch, that hurts!" I exclaimed.

She lightened the pressure but continued to hold the point.

I don't know how far into the session I was when Parnee said to stop the breathing and pound my legs and arms on the table. I felt awkward doing this at first. Here I am a grown woman having a fit like a little kid. But I reminded myself to be open to this as I did as she instructed. After about two minutes she told me to stop. That felt good, I thought. When it was time again to have another session of pounding my legs and arms, I relished it. I found it to be quite freeing.

Then came the point when Parnee applied pressure between my breasts. It's something I'll never forget.

I felt physical pain as she held this pressure point, but there was also this feeling of deep emotional distress that rose to the surface. It wasn't anything like I'd ever experienced before.

I was trying to hold it back but Parnee said, "What are you feeling right now?"

"I just want to cry as I feel this overwhelming sadness, but at the same time I feel like I want to scream."

"Keep breathing through this. Don't stop."

I wanted more than anything to stop at this point as it felt incredibly emotionally painful, but again Parnee encouraged me to keep going.

"Keep breathing, Barb. You can do this," she said in my right ear.

It was extremely intense, and even though I fought it at first, I stayed with it. Eventually, the intensity began to subside. As it did, I wondered, *What was that?*

That moment is still vivid to this day. I felt something shift within me. It was like this festering wound, so raw and primal, was now soothed with the most healing balm of love and warm light. A deep healing had occurred.

Parnee then coached me to slow my breathing and start to return to normal, then she gently propped me up with what I could only guess were many pillows behind my back. Eventually, she pulled the bolster from under my knees and instructed me to keep breathing normally.

"This is the final stretch of the session," she said quietly.

As I lay with my back supported, my knees bent and my feet resting on the table, I heard a song begin to play. I'd learn afterward it's called, *You Can Relax Now*, sung by Shaina Noll. As I lay there listening to the song, I saw myself in my mind's eye, at the age of six months old lying in an infant seat rocker. I was smiling and I was happy. What really struck me the most, though, was this overwhelming and deeply comforting feeling that I was safe and protected.

This song would continue to serve me positively as I moved through my integration phase, and I return to it often. I am grateful to the songwriter, Susan McMullen, for permitting me to share the lyrics, below:

> *You can relax now*
> *C'mon and open your eyes*
> *Breathe deeply now*
> *I am with you*
>
> *Oh my sweet sweet child*
> *Who do you think you are?*
> *You are the child of God*
> *And that will never change*

You had a dream, you misunderstood
You thought we were separate
But now you hear my voice and

You can relax now
C'mon and open your eyes
Breathe deeply now
I am with you

You are the love of my life
You are my one creation
You are eternity
And that will never change

You had a dream, you misunderstood
You thought we were separate
But now you hear my voice and
You can relax now
C'mon and open your eyes
Breathe deeply now
I am with you

You are the love of my life
You are my one creation
You are eternity
And that will never change

You can relax now
I am with you
You are the child of God
And that will never change

You can relax now
You are the child of God

As I listened to the song and continued to breathe, I was once again transported back to my infant self. Suddenly, I felt this incredibly warm, supportive, and loving energy swaddling me. I'd never experienced this before. Tears rolled down the side of my face. I felt God *with* me. It felt like I'd come home.

As another song played, I felt an even deeper knowing that I was changed.

As the second song ended, Parnee quietly said, "How are you doing, Barb?"

I whispered, "I feel like I'm floating on a cloud. I feel so loved."

"Continue to rest. I'm going to step out of the room and get you some water. I'll be back shortly."

"Okay."

I really didn't want to leave this space of what felt like unconditional love, while at the same time believed what I just experienced would always be with me. Slowly I began to move my arms, my legs, and my hands, and stretched as I opened my eyes.

It was then that I heard Parnee enter the room again. I turned my head to look at her as she handed me a bottle of water.

"Thank you."

"You're welcome. Is there anything you'd like to share regarding what you experienced?"

I paused for a few moments, gathering myself. The experience was still so close to the surface. I just wanted to weep, not out of sadness, but rather out of relief.

My voice cracked as I said, "I realized I was never alone. God had always been here with me."

Parnee smiled.

"It's hard to describe, but I just know now that I'm worthy. I've struggled with this for so long. But now I feel like I finally understand that I'm okay just as I am."

I softly laughed after I said that last sentence. "Funny, as this is what my dog Gidget was sharing with me through an animal communication session in February. She was trying to help me understand that she was fine as she is even though she has chronic bladder infections. But I just couldn't see it then and almost made a terrible mistake."

I paused for a few moments to take in what I'd just said as Parnee continued to hold space for me. "All I can say right now is, wow. I feel like everything is really going to be okay."

I was tired, but it wasn't that of exhaustion, but rather more like a deeply relaxed state. I slowly moved my legs over the side of the table and took my time to sit up.

"I really don't have much more to say. I just want to now silently relish the experience."

"That's understandable. It sounds like you moved through some pretty emotional feelings that needed to be worked on."

"I did, and it's all good. I should also get going. I have a long drive home."

"When you get home, to fully integrate what you've been through, continue to drink plenty of water. If you can, try not to do anything too strenuous and rest if you can. Also, don't go on the internet or watch TV."

"I'm absolutely going to honor that," I said. I moved off the table and walked to where my coat was hanging on a hook on the wall.

As I put my coat on I said, "Thank you so much, Parnee."

"You're welcome." She held open her arms she said, "May I give you a hug?"

"Of course," I said as I opened my arms and we embraced each other.

"Take good care, Barb."

As I walked through the door I said, "I will. Thank you again."

CHAPTER 29

Following the Signs

AS I LEFT Parnee's studio, I felt as though I was floating and not part of my body. I took my time walking to my car, taking in the calming sight of the tall evergreen trees around me. The sun was warm and there was a light breeze.

After I got into my car I just sat there for a few moments, gazing at the river that ran behind the trees as I mentally prepared myself for the drive back home.

I decided to take the backroads instead of the busy highway. I wanted to enjoy the signs of spring that were beginning to make themselves known—buds that were just starting to peek from the branches of trees and the grass slowly waking from its slumber.

As I drove down and around the winding roads I thought about how if we allow Spirit to guide us instead of trying to force how we *think* our life *should* go, we are brought to healing modalities such as I'd just experienced with Parnee. Suddenly, a feeling of gratitude overcame me that I had been led to learn about, and take part in, Transformational Breathwork.

I thought about how I'd been supported during these months of darkness and uncertainty. I never could have planned or predicted how it was all going to unfold. How often we are called to lean into our faith so that we may learn the reason for trying times, which, inevitably, is to remind us of what's truly important.

It's under the loving eye and care of Spirit that we are presented a pathway of healing through people, animals, and energetic and other modalities, if we are only open to the signs. How fortunate I've been to have many wise teachers, including those from the animal kingdom.

Time and again it's the reflective guidance from animals, Gidget among them, that have had the most profound impact on me. I remembered the first time I saw the photo of her on Petfinder.com and sensed something so very wise about her.

I've veered from my path of faith and gotten lost along the way. But each time I find my way back and am able to let go of a struggle; I find myself in a new state of grace I've not felt before.

When I arrived home, I was quite tired, but in a relaxed and surrendered way. The idea of my to-do list didn't appeal to me. I knew that honoring this time of integrating my experience from my time with Parnee was vital to my continued healing.

It can be difficult to put into words this unfolding of my path and what looking deeply at my emotional pain has meant. It's what I was *feeling* and this *knowing* that all the inner work I'd done to this point was my purpose of being here on this earth, though my mind often tried to convince me that I needed to be productive and *do* something. Now I knew I just had to allow myself to follow what felt right in any given moment, and that moment, when I arrived home, what felt right was rest.

As I lay down on the sofa my mind was still trying to understand what had occurred. But my heart knew I was changed in a new way. As I stared out the front door in this deeply relaxed state I thought there was no way I'd get back the energy to accomplish the tasks I had on my list for the following day.

The mind is such a curious thing, trying to convince us that we are missing out, or are perhaps even failures if we do not accomplish something every minute of every day. I had certainly been guilty of this, but for the time being I wanted to remain in this space of being. I trusted that I was safe, all would be well, and when it was time to move back into my daily tasks again, it would happen.

And it did. I was surprised when I awoke the next morning refreshed and rejuvenated. I was still feeling calm and centered within, but there was this newfound energy I had not felt in quite some time. I knew I had household and work tasks to accomplish, but I didn't feel hurried, or that everything had to be done in one day. I just knew that whatever needed to be done in this moment would be, and I would take care of what came next as it presented itself.

I walked into the kitchen to get a glass of water and smiled at a photo I have on the windowsill. It's a picture of one of my favorite authors, Tasha Tudor. Perhaps some may find it strange I keep a picture of an author I never met and who died in 2008 at the age of ninety-two years old.

It was serendipity that I discovered Tasha, who had lived in Vermont, two months before John and I left for a trip there. Initially I wanted to learn more about her because she was a children's author and illustrator and had a love for that short-backed and short-legged dog breed, the Corgi. But it was her philosophy on life that I'd feel a kinship with.

As the twenty-first century became more about consumerism and materialistic gain, Tasha never faltered from living the simple lifestyle she felt most at home in. She dressed in wool frocks, a scarf upon her head, and a shawl pinned around her shoulders. She looked straight out of the 1800s. In *Take Joy*, the documentary, she commented that when she died, she was quite sure she'd be going back to the 1800s, when she'd been married to a sea captain!

Like Tasha, I want more than anything to not get caught up in life's trappings. I want to live a simpler way of life and began to put this into practice over ten years ago.

The photo of Tasha in my kitchen, along with another picture of her in my writing cottage, are reminders that I too can choose a simpler life even if the world outside moves too quickly. My favorite *Tasha-ism* is one I heard her say in *Take Joy:* "I don't believe in hurry."

Some might think she was nuts; most might label her as eccentric, but there is something about her that I've always found grounding. It was her conviction in what she believed to be the truth for her life that to this day has me often returning to watch the documentary or reread the books written about her, which I have collected.

I'd come to realize that while my healing had much to do with letting go of the part of me that felt broken and was wounded, I'd also gotten trapped in what's sometimes referred to as FOMO—the fear of missing out.

My fifty-fifth birthday was on the horizon and I was having that familiar feeling that I've heard others talk about—that more of my life was now behind me than ahead. I'd also made projections about what I thought my life *should* be, mostly because of societal definitions of what the "good life" is, and how the media can wreak havoc on those who aren't living it.

Instead of encouraging us to think for ourselves and search our souls for what really matters to us individually, we often get sucked into a vortex of being part of the "in and happening" crowd. My ideal life may be entirely different than what it looks like for someone else, but that's perfectly okay. What matters is that we each live life on our terms and what we define as meaningful.

As I reflected on Tasha's quote, "I don't believe in hurry," I realized that when I've surrendered to the so-called pressures of the world, allowing my days to unfold as what feels right for me, I live in a reality that feels in alignment with my soul.

My feeling of kinship with Tasha is not an accident. The fact I never met her and that she is no longer living on this planet doesn't mean I don't know her and that she isn't part of me. It's what I feel about her way of life, her truth spoken and lived, that lights my heart up, and I know she is a guide for me.

The same has been true for the animals in my life. Though we don't speak the same language, they have time and time again served as a reflection of a part of me that needed to be healed. What a gift to be able to feel and live life in this way!

Even though I had still had those surreal moments, I trusted that this was part of the process. It couldn't be rushed. I needed to continue to allow everything to unfold within its own space of grace.

CHAPTER 30

Dreams

THE NEXT MORNING, dreams I'd had earlier in the year came unexpectedly to mind. I had never really been one to remember my dreams, or I would recall just a small fraction; therefore, I had rarely written them down or gave them much thought.

Most recently, though, I had become interested in how our dreams are able to offer us clues after attending a free monthly Dream Symposium hosted by transformational coach Jocelyn Mercado and dream analyst Tayria Ward. Tayria, as mentioned earlier, was the woman with whom Dawn had shared the story of my encounter with Snake.

There were many fascinating dreams shared during the symposium, which were then looked at and analyzed on a collective level. Hearing the insight Tayria and Jocelyn shared regarding a particular person's dream often left me in tears of understanding and awe. Since then, I had made a more conscious decision to pay attention to my own dreams and on occasion had written them down; it was one of these dreams that jumped into my mind this morning. I ran to find my journal as I couldn't remember the exact date of the dream and began flipping through the entries.

I'd had the dream on February 24, 2018, two days before Dawn had done the animal reading with Gidget. A shiver went up my spine. *Could there be a connection here?* After I read my notes about the dream, I sensed I knew what it might mean; I also knew I would need support to walk me through it. If I was correct about the dream's significance, it would be hard for me to be okay with it.

As I write this today, I am once again in awe of how we are truly guided along our life's journey. If it hadn't been for Dawn, I might not have come to know of Tayria and her work.

It was through the symposium that I came to trust and admire Tayria. Now it was time for me to reach out to her and ask for support. Again, I had a gut sense of what my dream was about, even though I also knew it would be painful to look at. But I'd come this far. I was ready.

I'm grateful that Tayria sensed the urgency of my email. Her schedule was quite full, but she graciously told me that if I needed to talk sooner, she would make it happen for me.

When we connected a few days later, she asked me to share the dream with her. I include the most significant part below.

> *A man took Dawn and me to a part of his basement where there was a small, narrow door. He told us that this is where he had his art and it was like a museum to get ideas. I noted it was eclectic and eccentric as Dawn and I looked around and the man went into what looked like his office. We kept walking down the hallway through small rooms, but then it got weird and creepy when I spotted what looked like blood spots on the ground—we were no longer walking on a path. It was as if we were outside now when we came upon a large dead dog laying halfway in the path. Dawn said to just walk around the dog, but I was scared and creeped out. We then came to what looked like wide tire tracks and in the tracks were blotches of dried blood. Looking past the dried blood, it was pitch black. I said I wanted to go back, but Dawn said the man would question us and not let us back out.*

After I was done reading my dream to Tayria, she said, "There's a lot there."

"I know," I said. "It's part of the reason I reached out for your help."

"Before I share my thoughts on the symbolism of your dream," she replied, "I'd like to know what you think it means."

I reminded her of my encounter with the dead snake and her suggestion to Dawn that there was something more there for me to work with.

"There was, and it helped me release the pain I had been carrying around since childhood."

She nodded in agreement.

"I know this encounter wasn't just an accident, especially given the fact that I've been experiencing so much anger and resentment the past few months. I believe this dream is also tied in some way to that same wound."

I could see how some of the symbolism in the dream spoke to a part of my psyche that I had sealed off to protect me from the hurt of the past. I could also clearly see that certain parts of the dream represented that specific wound, though it was hard to acknowledge.

I had learned through my studies over the years that dreams are part of the collective signs and symbols through which Spirit speaks to us. Our dreams are also part of our subconscious and often provide clues for us. I trusted that if I really looked inside this dream it would be another step toward freeing myself from the past and ultimately healing from it.

Tayria offered me suggestions about parts of my dream and what they may represent. The one that resonated for me the most was that the dead dog I saw in the road symbolized a loss of innocence. This helped me to feel safe in opening to the message little by little, understanding why I had blocked it due to fear and shame.

Tayria then asked if I wished to share the details of my childhood wound. Giving voice to those flashbacks and the details had been one of the most excruciating things I had ever done, but after receiving such loving support from Dawn, John and my mom, I now found it a bit easier. I no longer felt hostage.

Near the end of the session Tayria encouraged me to set aside time when I was ready and do a ceremony that felt right to me to completely release this pain from my past. She shared that it was important for me to also forgive and cut the cord.

I said," This feels right to me. I will absolutely take this step soon."

"Feel free to send me an email letting me know the day and time you plan to have the ceremony. I'll hold an energetic space of healing for you. You may want to ask Dawn to do the same."

What a beautiful thing to say, I thought. "Thank you so much, Tayria. I really appreciate this, and yes, I'll also contact Dawn when I'm ready."

Afterward, I sat staring out the window absorbing all that had transpired in such a short time. Indeed, much had been revealed in just an hour with Tayria. But I also recognized that it had taken a lifetime to get to this point.

I reflected on the day I talked to Dawn about my decision to put Gidget to sleep. I realized now how I'd convinced myself it was the right thing to do. But it was my projection of my own inner wound that was trying desperately to be heard.

Guilt and shame tried to flood my heart once again, but I knew I had to stay in this space of grace I had found my way to. I had to be grateful I hadn't followed through on that decision.

The battle that had been going on inside me for over two decades had reached the point where I couldn't think or see clearly, though I didn't recognize this as I was going through it. I recalled how I felt Dawn wasn't hearing or understanding me when I told her I'd made the decision to let Gidget go.

I also remembered how after we had gone back and forth for what felt like an eternity, Dawn said, "Barb, all I can say is I read energy, and I see a big black hole here."

Now it made perfect sense. While my nature is mostly one of being happy, positive, and optimistic, for much of my life there had been a part of me that was afraid to allow myself to truly feel my way through all my emotions—especially those I'd kept buried for fear they'd swallow me whole if I brought them to the surface and acknowledged them.

There was a time when I thought if I just practiced positive thinking all would be well. I still feel this is important as attitude certainly helps move us forward. But I've come to realize that when we don't allow and witness all our emotions, especially the difficult and painful ones, they are like poison that continues to swim through our veins.

As part of my healing ceremony, Tayria also suggested writing a letter expressing all the pain I'd felt for so long. It took me a few days to work up the courage to do this. But once the letter was written, I set the date to perform the ceremony.

I decided the ceremony would include reading the letter I wrote, forgiving what needed to be forgiven, and letting go of the past. I also emailed Dawn and Tayria with the time and date so they could hold an energetic space for me.

On a Friday morning two weeks later I set up an altar on a table in my writing cottage. In the center of the table I placed my fabric intuition snake doll; a small plastic snake I'd bought as a reminder of Snake's teaching; a white wolf totem named Laiola to symbolize the wolf who had come to me during the guided visualization three years before; an Angelite stone that symbolizes speaking the truth and aids in dispelling fear and anxiety; a rose quartz stone for compassion; a heart made out of stone as a reminder to open my heart fully; a small rock on which I had written the word "peace"; and a candle that I lit as I began the ceremony.

I also pulled an oracle card from *The Mystical Shaman Oracle* deck asking for guidance as I embarked on this ceremony. The deck, described as "a blend of mystical and shamanic wisdom," honors spiritual ideas of the deck's creators, Alberto Villoldo, Colette Baron-Reid and Marcella Lobos, and is a reminder that Oneness is the true nature of all things. The card I pulled was *Upper World*.

For me, the card was a reminder that I wanted to continue to rise above the shame, pain and guilt I'd kept buried. I felt strongly this was the path I was meant to travel to learn the lessons I needed to understand, but I was also ready to let go of the parts that no longer served me.

I then turned to the guidebook and *The Essence* message of the card. "*Angels, divine helpers, the Ancient Ones, and all varieties of luminous beings populate the upper world. It is the place where you go to retrieve your destiny and find out who you will become, discover your great potentials and undreamt-of possibilities. It is also the place where the spirits of the dead arrive when they complete their journey to the light.*"

The second part of the card's message, *The Invitation*, read: "*The upper world is calling you to step into your fully realized self. Clear distractions so that you can move into a higher destiny. Do not fall to the temptation to craft a slightly more improved version of yourself. What you perceive as a problem or an obstacle is, in fact, the irritation you need to take the great leap. Remember you cannot cross the Grand Canyon in two small jumps.*"

Every step I had taken over the course of my life, and in particular the intensity that had built over the past months, had led to this moment. I was more than ready to take this leap to release what had plagued me all these years. With tears running down my cheeks, I placed the oracle card next to my intuition doll. My altar was complete.

I took three deep breaths as I prepared myself to read the letter out loud. I read mostly from what I'd written, until anger rose to the surface. This prompted me to speak what the anger was about, along with more than a few swear words that made their way out my mouth. But I followed what felt right to express and allowed the anger to burst forth.

I did have a moment of doubt that I'd truly be able to forgive. But as I neared the end of the letter, I began to feel lighter in my body and spirit. I also knew I didn't want to fight this any longer. I wanted peace.

Reading the last sentence, I felt the anger subside as I sat for a time and just let all the emotions wash over me.

I inhaled another deep breath as I forgave the pain inflicted upon me. What surprised me, as it was not written in the letter, was when I heard myself give thanks for the teaching it provided. It was then I knew with an even stronger conviction that this had been *the path I had to walk* in order to arrive where I was now.

I'm not sure how long I sat staring out the window before I noticed it had begun to rain. How perfect, I thought. The rain was a symbol from the Universe that in holding this ceremony I was able to purify the pain and that it was now washing away into the earth.

Eventually, I stood up with the letter still in my hands, grabbed a lighter, and walked onto the deck. Placing the letter in the chiminea, I lit a corner of it and watched it burn.

I felt empty as I walked back to my writing cottage. But at the same time I felt light and a sense of deep comfort. I was going to be okay. I was safe. I was protected. I was loved. Most importantly, I was still me, but changed.

CHAPTER 31

Gidget's Reflection

AS I MOVED through the next few weeks with a new sense of stability and peace, I also noticed a substantial change in Gidget. Most days in the late afternoon, I'd sit on the sofa in the living room to catch up on newsletters and blogs I subscribe to. Gidget would often appear at my feet and hop up and down on her front limbs indicating she wanted me to pick her up. But lately, I noticed, she either continued to rest in her kennel in the kitchen or would take up residence in her bed next to the sofa.

At first I felt a bit hurt by this behavior. *Didn't Gidget want to be with me?* But I soon realized she was experiencing the same sense of peace that I was. This brought tears to my eyes, for I now understood how hard she had been diligently working to help me know what it was I needed to work through. And that she had never once given up on me.

All these months she had patiently waited for me to get on board and feel better about myself, and now that I had done the necessary inner work she could rest. I understood what a relief it was for her, as a big load had been lifted off my shoulders too. She was likely feeling the same.

I hadn't mentioned these changes to John, so when one evening he remarked how calm and different Gidget now seemed, I was surprised and overjoyed. It was such a sweet confirmation.

One day in late May, I was sitting on the deck with my friend Victoria, who had stopped in for a visit. We had been chatting for about a half hour when I realized Gidget was lying contently at the base of my chair. This was highly unusual, as she always had to be on my lap when I had friends over. My eyes misted over as I mentioned this to Victoria. It felt incredibly good to know Gidget was so much more relaxed these days.

I still had moments of guilt, though they were far less frequent. When this emotion surfaced I'd remind myself of the animal reading I'd had done with Gidget earlier that year. I remembered how Dawn shared with me that it was important for me to know that Gidget and I were meant to be together for both our needs/desires. The more I came into my own empowerment, the more she did too.

I reflected on how when I set out to adopt Gidget that I wanted more than anything for her to be my companion. I didn't want to share her with others in the way I had with Frankie. I wanted her all to myself.

I then thought back to 2006, when Frankie became paralyzed, and the period of transition she and I had gone through as we acclimated to her new needs. I also became more serious about my writing during that time, which led to the building of my writing cottage three years later. My world revolved around Frankie, writing books, visiting schools and libraries, and doing therapy dog work. Where I went, Frankie went. This also played out for a short while when Joie was in my life.

Gidget was a companion rather than a work partner, and thus I had learned to observe her differently. I'd come to realize how important it was to allow Gidget to be the dog she needed to be—not necessarily what I needed. For as long as I could remember, I had tucked a wiener dog under my right arm every morning and headed out to my writing cottage. To have a dog in my presence was always comforting and I enjoyed the companionship. *But was I really honoring Gidget's needs in doing this? Did she want to be with me all the time?*

I decided to let her make her own choice. Each morning, instead of scooping her under my arm as I usually did, I'd stand at the patio door and call for her. During the warm months she often chose to answer my call and come to lie on the deck. As fall approached and the days grew cooler, however, her choice was to stay tucked warmly in her bed inside the house.

I admit I missed her companionship as I worked in my writing cottage. But I came to appreciate the alone time for meditation time and journaling with my oracle cards before I dove into my work for the day.

Thinking back, I realized how often she couldn't seem to settle in next to me as I meditated in my wicker chair. This was frustrating for both of us. Now that I was valuing the space she needed, rather than forcing her to be with me, the more I came to see the gift she'd given me.

This had me thinking in an expanded way about our relationships with our pets. I've come to believe on an even deeper level that the reason animals share this planet with us is that they are trying to get our attention and get us do the essential inner healing work that most of us need to do in some capacity.

I realized how we often project our emotional needs onto our pets and cause them needless suffering. The fact that this is often done subconsciously only makes it more deserving of serious thought and consideration. We are here to learn the lessons that will help our souls evolve, and many animals agree to facilitate this journey. Helping us to see our deeper selves is the true essence of their teachings.

For me, this is evidenced by what I experienced with Gidget, who walked so lovingly beside me as I opened to the deep pain I'd carried for so long. Though it felt incredibly vulnerable, and painful, to share the resentment and anger I felt toward her, it also served as my wakeup call that something needed to be healed. Gidget was giving me an opportunity to enhance my life by facing my inner wounding and working through it, which in turn benefitted Gidget and John as well.

I still sometimes shuddered at the thought that I almost missed out on gaining this deeper insight, not to mention having Gidget here with me. But I was also grateful for the way Gidget came into my life and the journey we walked together. I recalled with some awe the first time I saw her picture and sensed there was something very wise about her, though I would only recently understand the true depths of that wisdom. She truly was my Buddha Dog.

CHAPTER 32

Grace Becoming

AS 2018 WAS coming to a close, I started to give thought to my word for 2019. It was an exercise I had started in 2017 as a way of setting an intention for the year ahead.

That first year, my word was *Magical*, a choice inspired by two books I had read—*Magical* by Elizabeth Gilbert and *Still Writing* by Dani Shapiro—both of which are about the creative life. I appreciated the fact that they spoke to owning and standing in one's truth as a vital component to a deeply satisfying life.

Elizabeth and Dani indeed forged their own paths and didn't buy into the so-called "shortcuts to creativity" we are so often bombarded with via social media and marketing tactics. I understood this completely, as in the first few years of my creative life, especially after Frankie passed away, I had found myself feeling burnt out from thinking I should do things a certain way.

It was only after taking my sabbatical in 2013 that I was determined to live a creative life on my own terms, even if that meant I failed at times. After all, is there really such a thing as failure? I don't think so. I've come to see "failure" as what I needed to learn in order to guide me to the next phase of my life.

In 2018 I couldn't seem to settle on just one word and chose two instead—*Abundant* and *Depth,* the latter to express my desire to experience more in-depth conversations with others. Now that I was on the other side of what had been a very challenging year, I realized how profound these choices had been, and that it was not only about my communication with others, but with myself. Indeed, more than ever before I had spent the last year focusing inward and truly listening, feeling, and breathing in the truth of my soul. And in doing so I was able to heal a painful wound, integrate it, and let it go. Most importantly, I came to understand again that this journey, though exceedingly painful, was essential as it helped shape who I am.

Now, as 2019 approached, I decided my word should honor Gidget for her teachings, and for myself for having the courage to take this deep dive into my inner world. That said, I didn't want to force anything but to just allow it to unfold. I didn't have to wait too long, for one night in mid-December, Spirit nudged me awake. Two days prior I'd received an unexpected gift in the mail from Cass, a woman who had been following me since my work with Frankie.

Enclosed in the envelope was a beautiful postcard. The message on the back read, "I listened to your wonderful interview on *The Wiener Dog Lover* podcast. I was touched by how our beloved companions teach us so much. Spirit guided me to send you a copy of Miranda Macpherson's book, *The Way of Grace*. The themes seem to resonate so much with what you share."

She also included a replica of a painting she called *Somewhere over the Rainbow Bridge*. It was a portrait of little dachshunds in heaven, some of them in wheelchairs. I especially loved that. After Frankie passed away, many had shared with me their belief that in heaven Frankie was free to walk again without the aid of her wheelchair. But I never saw Frankie in that way on the other side. I'd come to see those wheels not just as a tool but as *part* of her; they made her who she was.

As I held the book in my hands I silently asked what it was I most needed to know at the moment, and randomly opened to a page. It was this line that got my attention:

> *Compassion is a manifestation of Grace, and Grace always comes forward when you surrender, relax and just be here—with nothing to fix or get or do. Feel your feet on the earth and your body held by the chair as you meet any concerns or overwhelm.*

This past year I had indeed been brought to my knees as I struggled to try and *fix* the emotional roller coaster I had been on. But it was in truly surrendering that I was guided by this force I had always believed in but had never really *felt* until recently. The more I leaned into this and followed my threads of intuition, the more the overwhelm dissipated.

It was in learning to have more empathy for myself that I was actually able to see through the eyes of compassion more often. The more I experienced this, the more it felt divinely graceful.

As I lay in bed in the early morning hours thinking about signs that had come my way of late, I remembered another book I'd recently been gifted by my friend Monica—*Return to Grace* by Cheryl Richardson. I had actually read it years before, but knew it was no coincidence that Monica had now been called to pass on to me a used copy she'd picked up at her church.

Just then, the words *Grace Becoming* came to the forefront of my mind. My right hand flew to my chest and rested on my heart. I realized these would be my words for 2019.

Grace Becoming represents for me the adage that we are all a work in progress. We are never "finished" so long as we walk this earthly plane. The more I reflected on the quote I opened to at random in Miranda's book, the more I felt at my core the words *grace becoming* are really about compassion, starting with the compassion we must first learn to have toward ourselves.

We've gotten so caught up in this idea of perfection and thinking others have better lives than we do that we end up believing we are alone in our struggles. We also fear making mistakes. I can certainly attest to having these feelings, and more than I sometimes care to admit.

But it's cultivating compassion *first* with ourselves that we need to practice. This requires taking time each day to be in touch with what matters to our souls and to understand that at a core level we all want the same things—to feel loved, heard, and to experience peace.

Grace Becoming is my gentle reminder that I will always be a work in progress and to lovingly embrace this. The more I practice compassion for myself, the more grace I experience not only in myself, but reflected in the world around me. Each and every day I have the opportunity to become, and welcome in, more grace.

CHAPTER 33

Animal and Oracle Wisdom

IT WAS LATE November when I'd be invited to practice *Grace Becoming* yet again.

The Saturday after Thanksgiving as I was decorating my home for Christmas I noticed Gidget didn't seem herself. She had never walked perfectly well, having that little giddy-up to her gait because of her IVDD, but now she was having more difficulty than usual in getting around. She also seemed a bit lethargic, rather than displaying her usual spunk. I was worried something was wrong, though she had no visible signs of pain. I kept a close eye on her.

On Sunday morning she wasn't walking. I carried her to her food bowl, where she ate her breakfast with her usual gusto. Dogs with IVDD can have flare-ups or additional discs that give them trouble, and though I didn't sense this was the case with her I knew I needed to make an appointment with the vet. I made a mental note to call the next morning.

As I observed her throughout the day, I thought perhaps something may be going on with her digestive system because her belly appeared bloated to me. I was able to get her in first thing Monday morning. Upon examination, Dr. Mary didn't feel it was a digestion issue.

Gidget had gained some weight which I knew wasn't good, especially being an IVDD dog. As she has aged, she isn't as active anymore either. Dr. Mary did an exam of her spine and concluded that nothing was out of the ordinary. Nothing conclusive was found. I agreed that Gidget needed to lose some weight, though something still felt off to me. But I had more peace of mind having had her examined by the vet.

The next afternoon, when Gidget and I woke from a nap on the sofa, I smelled a foul odor. Initially I thought she'd had a bowel movement, but then I realized the towel beneath her was soaked with urine.

I was sure she had a bladder infection. I called the vet office right away and got her in for a needle aspiration. Indeed, this is what we were dealing with yet again. We were ending the year as we began it. Typical protocol treatment of antibiotics for Gidget was fourteen days, but this time Dr. Mary prescribed a twenty-one-day treatment.

As I drove home, a part of me was relieved to know Gidget would soon be feeling better. But then familiar feelings of frustration rose to the surface. Before I knew it, I began that familiar descent down the rabbit hole. *How could I have missed the signs? What could I do so this did not keep occurring?* I worried again about the financial costs and then started thinking about how unfair this was to Gidget and me. At one point I said out loud, *Seriously Spirit, are we having to go through this yet again?*

The next morning I was still berating myself for what I thought I could have done better. I recognized that my mind was on a familiar loop of inwardly punishing myself and immediately flashed back to my dark night of the soul earlier in the year. It was then I knew I needed to be with all that I was feeling.

As I meditated, the tears I'd been holding back finally released and ran down my face. I realized once again that when I feel inadequate, I'm coming from that wounded place within me. I feel constricted, trapped, and helpless, and unleash an endless stream of criticism on myself, which only magnifies the angst.

I then thought about all the measures I had taken with regard to Gidget's care, from working with my local vet and bringing her to see a holistic vet and acupuncturist, to getting her Chinese Herbs and other bladder supplementation, and keeping her clean. It was then a light bulb went on, and I saw this in a way I'd not before. I was doing *all I could* to support her.

After my meditation, as I often do, I decided to pull oracle cards around this situation to see what further insight I could gain.

The first card I pulled from *The Wisdom of the Oracle* was *Truth Be Told*. I immediately saw the card reflecting that the truth was that I'd fallen back into the same trap again. When things go astray in my life, I fall back into the pattern of blaming myself and thinking I'm not good enough.

As I stared at the card a while longer, I recalled the interview I'd recently done on *The Wiener Dog Lover* podcast. At one point during the interview, I'd shared with the host, Lori, how frustrated I'd become earlier in the year when Gidget had yet another bladder infection. I talked about how this had escalated to the point that I felt like I'd lost all coping skills. As I shared this with her, I could still clearly feel the great deal of angst I had suffered just seven months prior.

I was quite taken aback when I heard Lori chuckle. Because this was a phone interview, she couldn't see me, but I felt my body clench into that constricted place again.

She said, "I didn't mean to laugh, it's just that those of us who have dachshunds with IVDD know how common bladder infections are and how dachshunds are one of the hardest breeds to potty train."

She wasn't laughing *at* me, nor was she trying to diminish what I'd gone through earlier in the year; she was merely acknowledging that such a common issue had been the catalyst to my hitting rock bottom. The blessing was that it ultimately helped me to step from behind a mask of shame, pain, and guilt stemming from a wounding in my youth that had played out as a pattern and had often kept me imprisoned within myself.

Lori's innocent chuckling was yet another reminder that while what I was going through with Gidget was certainly frustrating, I could choose not to carry it as a burden. I didn't need to hide behind a mask of pretending that I wasn't tired sometimes but could instead face my feelings and express them. The more I journaled, the more the tears flowed, bringing me a welcome release. This eventually allowed more peace to enter.

The next card I pulled was *Snake Spirit* from the *Spirit Animal Oracle* deck. The front of the card read, *Time to heal.*

I immediately flashed back to the dead mama snake and her four babies I had seen lying just past my driveway three years earlier. It had been my willingness to see this not as a mere coincidence but something that touched me deep inside, that had me reach out to Dawn and learn what message Snake had for me. Having "Danced with Snake" back then, I was now able to recognize that I was being presented with yet another opportunity for healing.

As I sat staring at the picture of the snake on the card, I heard that part of me that still felt I was somehow not where I thought my life *should be*, instead of just being with *what is.*

I was putting myself in victim mode when I carried this attitude and projecting into the future of "what ifs." Snake was inviting me once again to shed another layer, to be with all my tender emotions, honor how far I'd come, and to see that each time I felt burdened to look at it as an opportunity to go straight to the root of why.

After journaling my thoughts, I picked up the guidebook that accompanied the cards. The line that brought it all home for me was, "*Unburden yourself of anything that no longer supports wellness, prosperity, positive relationships, and well-being, and open the door for healing to occur.*"

It was then that the quote from the book, *The Way of Grace* practically sang out to me:

> "*Compassion is a manifestation of Grace, and Grace always comes forward when you surrender, relax and just be here—with nothing to fix or get or do.*"

Just as I couldn't' fix or change my past wounding, I realized I also couldn't fix Gidget. But when I could surrender and relax into *what is*, peace found me and grace could then lead the way.

CHAPTER 34

Out of the Shadows

AS I PONDERED how to invite more grace into my life, I reflected on the e-newsletter I had sent to my followers back in May.

I had not been able to write much during the winter months while going through my deep emotional work. At times this was difficult because a part of me felt obligated to stay in touch with those who had followed my work all these years. But I was also building a trust in myself to keep on the path of healing that would positively serve me in the long run.

Writing to my followers three months later, the title of my newsletter was: *Out of the Shadows. A Call to Life.*

It was early spring, a time often associated with rebirth. In the newsletter, I reflected on my appreciation for nature and the way it so beautifully reflects the seasons of rebirth we will periodically go through. I had certainly been going through such a period, and I wanted my followers to know that this was the reason for my absence.

I shared the angst, chaos and darkness I'd been through the past few months, and what it felt like as I faced a wounding from my childhood.

It was important to me to let my followers know that all emotional pain matters, regardless of the details of our individual stories. I wanted them to know what I'd come to understand on a more intimate level—that our pain and deep hurts are signposts, guiding us to see them for what they are, to integrate them, release them, and open to a new way of witnessing ourselves. No matter our past, we are each beautiful and caring souls with the power to create fulfilling lives.

I learned that by lovingly exploring my soul, I was not only granted more compassion for myself, I also opened a deeper channel of empathy. It was a gift to remember to be more mindful of those walking beside me who likely have fears of their own.

It was seeing myself through the reflection of my dog, Gidget, that allowed me to open to parts of myself I had never allowed myself to look at before. Though it was still difficult to do, I came to appreciate, honor, and love those parts for loving and protecting me. And it was in facing a difficult memory that I was able to come out of the shadows grateful for another opportunity at this wild and precious life.

A few days after I sent the newsletter update, a vision flashed across my mind; it was one I'd had seen several times in meditation over the past few years. Now, though, I realized it had been a while since I'd had it.

In it, I am sitting on a beach and wearing a wide-brimmed straw hat that partially covers my face. My legs are pulled up in front of me with my feet and toes buried in the warm sand. Gidget is on my lap with her front legs and paws resting on my thighs, and my arms are wrapped around the front of my knees holding her in place.

We are there together looking out over the water as a time of reflection and connection. It's peaceful, and I don't want to leave that space of contentment.

Now, as I realized the significance of this familiar vision, tears formed in my eyes. It would be the inspiration for the image I'd end up choosing as the cover of this book. The only difference is that in the cover photo my straw hat is not covering my face; in fact, my contented expression is clearly visible, as is Gidget's.

Gidget and I are also faced away from the water and looking out into the world. I see with clarity now the wise teacher Gidget is as she sits in front of me in such an astute and confident way. And I see myself as the woman who can say with more conviction than before that this is who I am too.

When I think back to first finding, and then adopting Gidget, I can see now the gifts she brought me. There were so many signs along the way that I was being guided to a new understanding of self and my relationship with Gidget, though these weren't always easy to interpret. I often felt frustrated and confused at times, but now when I look back I have clarity.

Now I see that when we make a conscious choice to live with more awareness, we are granted more opportunities to sense and experience the world around us in a deeper way.

I remember when Cheryl, the head of the rescue from which I adopted Gidget, told me that Gidget had come from a woman she defined as a "pretty dog collector," who then surrendered Gidget when she was no longer perfect. Though I had never heard this term before, it struck a nerve; however, it was only when I revisited it later from a new perspective that I saw another opportunity to shed another layer of emotional pain I carried.

While growing up I had often been told I was pretty by friends, co-workers, acquaintances, and family. While they meant it as a compliment, there were times it was confusing and played havoc with my self-esteem.

Just as it does now, our culture back then placed an emphasis on youth and beauty and correlated them with "having it all." Paradoxically these compliments created in me a deep feeling of not good enough, as well as a determination that I somehow had to keep on top of and maintain my looks.

For most of my life I didn't like it when men looked at me, though I did all I could to look my best. This too may sound odd, as if I was trying to call attention to myself while at the same time not wanting the attention. But it was all I knew, even though I considered myself shy and an introvert.

As it would turn out, my appearance also brought a different kind of attention that was even more disconcerting. I was working as a visual merchandiser at a big department store—my first full-time job out of college—and was excited to learn that I had won a workplace contest. My excitement turned to sadness when a few days later a co-worker told me that another co-worker—and a good friend of mine—had remarked that I had only won the contest because I was pretty.

I was deeply hurt by that remark, especially since the friend knew how hard I had worked on the contest. I never asked her about it and chose to never talk to her again. It was the only way I knew how to deal with it at the time -walk away from her and bury the feelings it incited around my looks.

There was also another time when a guy told me that if I just lost a few pounds I'd be prettier—also hurtful, though in a different way.

On some level, these feelings were triggered when Cheryl made the comment about the "pretty dog collector." As everyone knows by now, dachshunds are my favorite breed and even among them Gidget could be considered quite a beauty. But it was the soulful connection I felt with her, from the first time I saw her photo, that made me want to adopt her. It was the same thing I'd felt when I initially saw Joie and adopted her in 2012. While I couldn't say exactly why, I just knew in my heart Gidget was the one.

Now, as I reflected on my earlier life challenges, as well as those I had faced with Gidget, I realized how interconnected they were. I recalled the early, and thankfully false, scares around her heart, followed by that chilly January evening a little over a year after we adopted her when Gidget suffered her first seizure.

It took another ten months before we had Gidget's seizures under control with medication and after December 2015 she never had another seizure. But it was an exhausting and frustrating time. I remember one day at the height of it all coming home from grocery shopping to find Gidget was not herself. She was pacing, and I tripped over her a few times because she kept getting underfoot as I tried to put the groceries away.

After putting the food away, I'd gone out to my writing cottage to do some work. When I returned a little while later, Gidget was chewing apart a rug. While she was an anxious dog from the day she came to live with us, things seemed to be escalating, and now this. At times, I was so tired from what I perceived this "high strung" ball of energy that could never quite calm down.

Now, as I look back and all Gidget and I have gone through, I believe deep in my heart, and with what I've come to understand about energy, that she had taken on the energy of my childhood wounding I'd kept buried all these years.

At one time I might have been skeptical about this, but now I simply cannot see it any other way. It would be seven months after Gidget's first seizure that I gave voice to the wounding that haunted me. I still recall how it came forth so unexpectedly, and as if it wasn't really me speaking. But yet, *it was me.*

As I began to slowly acknowledge that pain over the next months and years, it led me to hit rock bottom with the frightening thought that I'd rather die than deal with the pain. But eventually through the support I received, and being honest about all my feelings, I came to find myself in this new lighter and freeing energetic space. Most remarkable was the positive change in Gidget, who became so much calmer and not the same dog as when she first came to live with us. It was all the proof I needed.

I believe with all my being that Gidget came into my life to help me face and deal with one of the toughest things I've ever endured but that which was crucial in order for me to evolve.

It was in witnessing her newfound contentedness and being more comfortable in her own skin, that I felt my heart expand in deep appreciation for this gift she had given me.

Over the last thirteen years I had shared my life with three dachshunds, each with her own personality, each with unique teachings she provided me. Frankie taught me how to see challenges in a positive way and begin to gain confidence in myself, which had been sorely lacking. Joie taught me how to embrace change and transitional times in my life. And Gidget taught me that with inner focus I could heal a long-held wound, and that it's okay to be gentle and kind, but deep and true, too.

In many ways, I feel I've come full circle from Frankie and my first memoir, to Joie and my second memoir, to now Gidget and this memoir. As of this moment it feels like it will be my last. While I can't say that for sure (as I continue to be a work in progress) this part of my journey does feel complete to me, thanks in large part to a loving husband, good friends, and three amazing dachshunds.

The animals in particular, including Snake and the white wolf, have been reflections for me and what I needed to heal. They've shown me that by seeing life sideways, I've been gifted with perspectives I'd likely not have gleaned otherwise.

My fascination with metaphysics, oracles, animal wisdom, and the mystical continue to grow as a way in which feels right for me as I continue to walk this earthly journey. The more I open to observing everything around me as an oracle—a form of communicating not only with myself but in connection with the Divine—the more I feel supported and safe.

As I gave thought to the blessings I've received through living with three disabled dachshunds, I wondered about the symbolism of the number three and whether there was a worth delving into.

Referring to a book called *Messages in the Numbers—The Universe is Talking to You* by Alana Fairchild, I read the chapter on the symbolism of the number three.

I resonated with the number three being all levels of wellbeing coming together via physical, emotional and spiritual, as each dachshund represented helping me with a healing aspect for me of each.

It also talks about how the number three may have a message for those who feel tired, but that it does not necessarily mean that one does not have enough energy. Rather, the energy may be scattered, causing us to feel depleted. When I think back to how fatigued I felt the last few years, often expressing how tired and exhausted I was, to the marked shift I now feel, this resonates also.

The last few years I often needed a nap many days, but today I don't need them nearly as often. I have no doubt that the burden of a long-held wound I'd kept inside contributed to the exhaustion I'd been feeling.

The chapter also states that three is about a new life beginning. In many ways, this does feel like a new beginning for me, especially since there are times when I don't know exactly what the next step of my journey will be. When feelings of uncertainty arise, I remind myself that when I surrender and allow my life to unfold as it's meant to, I trust with more conviction that I'm being guided.

CHAPTER 35

No Place Like Home

AS I BEGAN to write this chapter, a familiar song began to play: Jon Schmidt's "Prelude (To My Little Girl" from the album, *To the Summit*). I took a moment to look at the cover and I saw in the design the shape of a female lion. I smiled, as just moments before I'd pulled oracle cards for my daily journaling, and the card I received was lion.

It wasn't an *actual* lion I saw on the cover of the album, but it was what *I* saw. I realized it was for good reason. I had woken at four a.m. and while still lying in bed, I recalled a day a few years ago when I was spending time with my mom. I remembered how it felt like it was out of the blue when I started to cry and told her why I had never wanted children. I was deathly afraid of the pain a baby would cause while coming out of my body.

As I thought about that memory, the little girl in me that was just too afraid to have children faced the deeper aspect of my wounding. I found myself crying over the loss that I'd never birth a child. It was something I had avoided thinking about and blocked it from coming to the surface.

I'd thought I'd made a conscious choice to not have children, but it was really my subconscious, the wounded little girl within that had been protecting me. Through the mama lion I saw shapeshift on that album cover, and the lion oracle card I'd pulled for the day, I had received another piece of the puzzle. I was the fierce and protective lioness doing what needed to be done to protect her cub—and that cub was *me*.

As I sat with the pain and grief, I eventually arrived at a place of acceptance and understanding that this was part of my soul's evolution and what I was to learn in this life. I realized if I chose to remain in regret or grief, I'd continue to carry that burden with me. I stared up at the ceiling as tears slid down my cheeks, knowing I could release this next level of pain, bring it fully into my being, and transcend it.

As I began to feel lighter in mind and spirit, releasing and integrating what I'd learned from my recent dark night of the soul, I marveled at how my home had begun to shape itself to reflect my new state of being.

Home has always been important to me. It's my sanctuary, my safe place to land. Now, as John and I remodeled the kitchen and living room, I clearly saw how the changes we were making were a reflection of inner lightness I was feeling.

In thinking about this, I was led to revisit the journal I'd kept since going through personal mastery and beginning my daily practice of pulling and reflecting upon oracle cards. I reread the entry from November 18, 2018, which was around the time my home was taking on its new look.

The card I had pulled that day was *No Place Like Home*. Oh, how my heart flooded with warmth when I saw it!

I wrote: *This card definitely represents how my heart feels right now. I'm relishing in following the flow and feeling so at home in my heart with the transformation of my living room.*

As I looked at the beam of light radiating out from the photo of the home on the card I heard, *Let that feeling residing in your heart right now radiate out into the world.*

When I turned to the guidebook to see if there was additional insight, this paragraph spoke to me: *This card signals that your ability to trust yourself and feel at home in your own skin is beginning to solidify as you claim your dignity and integrity, aspects of yourself no one can take away from you.*

It was true. For so long I hadn't trusted or believed in myself. The more I accepted the journey I had to walk in order to learn the lessons I needed to learn, the more I understood this was what had helped shape who I am. Without it, would I have been the same person?

Next, I drew a card from *The Spirit Animal Oracle* deck as my animal ally for the day and pulled *Vulture Spirit*. The message on the front of the card read, *Nothing is wasted.*

I wrote this in my journal: *All the roads I've traveled—especially the difficult ones or when it felt like life was standing still—all were part of the process to bring me back home to my heart once again. It all mattered to get to this deeper place of understanding.*

The passage in the guidebook that rang true for me was, *No pain was in vain, and no experience was wasted, for you have the power to use it to co-create something far better.*

As I continued to integrate the deep healing I'd been through, signs of support continued to present themselves. One day as I was listening to an interview with Tosha Silver, author of *Outrageous Openness, Let the Divine Take the Lead*, I heard her say, "You can't release something until you deeply feel it."

All the shame, resentment and anger I'd repressed all those years eventually manifested in a way I could have never predicted. The growing frustration I felt toward that sweet creature, Gidget, would have only continued to escalate had I not agreed, and then found a way, to explore all my feelings on a deep level.

By facing my own wounding, everything shifted. What once felt like a poor quality of life, when seen "sideways" as Gidget encouraged me to do, became a life full of opportunities for healing and joy that radiated to everyone I interacted with.

CHAPTER 36

Loyalty

BY THE BEGINNING of January, I had begun to focus most of my energy on completing this book. The words were flowing with so much more ease as I anticipated this project coming to a close.

Indeed, I woke most mornings thinking about where I'd left off writing the day before, followed by what it was I wanted to write next. That said, moving through my morning routine was important for centering myself before my fingers hit the keyboard.

I had made a small but significant adjustment to this routine; instead of pulling oracle cards after my yoga practice like I usually did, I was pulling them first thing. I wanted to be with their energy and ponder their meaning as I moved through my yoga practice.

As I sat at the table in my writing cottage, I pulled *Soul Mates and Beaver Spirit*. As sometimes happens, I didn't have a clue as to what these cards meant, at least in relation to my life. I laid them on the table and began my yoga routine.

Near the end of my practice, I was in downward facing dog when I was suddenly overcome with emotion. I found myself saying out loud, *I love you Gidget. I love you so much. Thank you.* I was surprised when I heard myself say this. It felt like it came from out of nowhere.

As I ate my breakfast, I thought about how my teaching from Gidget continued to deepen into my being. The more I integrated this experience of moving through a dark time to the lightness I now felt, my gratitude for her was growing more profound.

It was then I opened to my Facebook page to see I had a message from my friend Missy. She'd sent me a short video titled, "Loyal dog walks slowly with an elderly owner."

The clip shows an old man hunched over, slowly walking down the sidewalk as the sound of traffic whooshes in the background. There is a cane in his right hand and in his left hand, a leash. As the camera travels downward, you see the see the leash is attached to a red dachshund, a faithful companion who walks at the same pace as his beloved friend.

Missy wrote, "So much symbolism here for you, Barb."

I had seen this video before, but now it had a whole new meaning.

My eyes misted over as I once again recalled the animal reading I had done almost a year ago with Gidget. It was during that reading when Gidget shared that though her body may not be quick she was in her wisdom. She also shared that she was continuing to come into her higher self. I now understood with even more clarity that she had been encouraging me to do the same.

As I watched the video, I sensed on yet another level that Gidget was indeed my reflection of the importance of slowing down and working on the details of my inner world. For a while I had lost my way, and I had to go within and work on healing the wound in order to evolve into the next phase of my life.

What really struck me was that she never gave up on me.

Reflecting on the oracles cards I pulled earlier I realized that the *Soul Mates* card was speaking to my relationship with Gidget. I thought, *She truly is my soulmate at this time in my life, guiding me to be my best self.*

Turning to the guidebook, it read: *"This is the kind of soul mate who comes with a powerful gift. Your patterns and all your old stories that don't serve your well-being enter into this dynamic so you can heal them. This person is called to a sacred task—to help you learn, even if it seems uncomfortable. Look into this mirror. You will only be changed for the better."*

I smiled through tears as I felt the profound truth of this. The world is filled with oracles and symbolism as guides, and one of the greatest of these for me has been animals.

As I neared the completion of my book, writing an ending felt challenging. I wanted to be sure I captured all I wanted to share, in keeping with my hope that my story would help others. A part of me also didn't want this part of the journey to be done, though I knew in my heart I was ready to move on.

After my writing session for the day, I posted a photo of myself staring out the window on Instagram. I shared with my followers that I was in contemplation mode. A friend commented with one simple word: *closure*.

It didn't feel like closure to me, though, but more like integration. As I honored just accepting where I was, and not trying to force the process, I realized once again the many moments we must take to pause and integrate experiences we feel changed by.

If we don't take time to allow the flow of integration with all we've learned, we can be left hanging in emotional limbo. It's in quiet times with a conscious connection to our hearts that we need to reflect and *feel* our way through, that grace enters, and we are granted a feeling of completeness and wholeness.

It was the same for this project that I needed to honor my need just to be and allow the timing to unfold as it was meant to. It would be two days later when I'd receive a call that shook my world.

CHAPTER 37

Full Circle

WHEN MY CELL phone rang around noon on Friday, I recognized the name as that of Jen, the daughter of my dear friend, Marie. She was calling to tell me that Marie had passed away the day before. This was a shock, for though Marie had recently been diagnosed with terminal cancer I thought with treatment she would be here for quite some time. I couldn't believe she was gone.

Though I had only known her for about six years, "Miss Marie," as I lovingly called her, had a profound impact on my life. Marie was a talented fiber artist, and I marveled at her confidence and no-nonsense spirit. She dressed in a manner that I'd define as eclectic with a splash of eccentricity and an artistic twist. She was definitely someone who lived by the beat of her own drum. I was working hard to do the same and saw her as a role model. She also had a healthy sense of humor and enjoyed my nickname for her so much that had taken to calling me Miss Barbara and Gidget, Miss Gidget. Oh we were quite the trio!

After a hiatus from her art, she began to sell her exquisitely designed pillows and bags at our local Farmers and Artisans Market. I purchased one of her pillows with a dragonfly design, and I was deeply honored when Marie told me it was I who'd encouraged her to sell her artwork.

Two days later I was walking by Marie's house and saw her outside. I stopped to chat and she told me about a dragonfly that had landed on her porch a few hours after I bought the pillow. She told me that she didn't recall this ever happening before.

"I was quite sure it was you, Miss Barbara," she said, "coming to thank me for the pillow!"

This endeared her to me even more because she saw the unfolding of life in the same way as I did. It also set the stage that would expand into deep conversations about spirituality as I grappled with my understanding of God. Marie never judged me but was always open to hearing my thoughts.

Now nothing seemed to matter as I swam in the grief of knowing I'd never see my dear friend again. Marie was always supportive of my writing, and I wondered what the point was of continuing with it, though by that point I was nearing the completion of the second draft of my manuscript. Indeed, losing her made me wonder if there was any point to life at all.

One day shortly after her passing, I filled the kitchen sink with water and dish soap and began washing the dishes by hand. It was something I rarely did but it felt oddly comforting now as I gazed out the window and fond memories of Marie flashed through my mind. It was then I recalled what my best friend Victoria had said to me when I called to tell her the news:

"She was your own Tasha Tudor."

Marie had indeed reminded me of Tasha, who had also lived by the beat of her own drum.

I felt called to watch yet again *Take Joy*, the documentary about Tasha I mentioned earlier, as a way of honoring Marie's life. As I watched it, soaking in Tasha's philosophy on life, I felt an even deeper connection between the two women. Both artists, with a twist of eclectic eccentricity who lived a simpler life and didn't believe in hurrying.

The next morning as I walked into the kitchen, I glanced at the altar I'd made with my favorite photo of Marie and Gidget. I then looked at the calendar on the wall. The following evening friends and family would gather to celebrate Marie's life; I also noted March 4, the date of her funeral.

Suddenly, I heard a voice say, "march forth." I was sure this was a sign from Marie that I must move forward with my life. She would always be a part of me.

It was destined in the stars that we become friends. She was a reflection of what I'd wished to become, and now am. The best way in which I can honor her and all she taught me, and showed me through her beautiful example, is to continue to live by the beat of my own drum and be that example for those who yearn to do the same.

CHAPTER 38

Closure

AFTER ATTENDING MARIE'S funeral, I found myself circling back to the word closure. Recently, I listened to an interview with author Richard Rohr, who has written many books on spirituality. I resonated with what he said about the word evolve: that just the mention of it frightens many people because we are so afraid of change.

To me, if we seek closure, we miss out on the expanding and evolving of our souls. To grow, we have to be willing to be with our emotional pain. It teaches us something about ourselves. It's what helps shape us.

We are always in some stage of moving toward, and then into, our evolved selves as we walk this earthly plane. I don't believe we are ever complete, and thus there is no closure. There is instead an invitation to continue to expand and become.

One of my favorite oracle cards, though it wasn't when I first encountered it, is *Never-ending story* from *The Wisdom of the Oracle*. Whenever that card presents itself in my personal readings, I know it's a clue to look at where I'm getting stuck and repeating patterns from the wounded part of myself. I now know it's an opportunity to grow beyond the place I find myself stuck in.

Indeed, I've learned a great deal about looking into the darkness of my soul and working with what caused me so much angst and heartache. I know now that the path that helped shape me into who I am came with darkness so I could appreciate the light. To take away the darkness would be like a piece of my soul is missing. *All* of it makes me who I am.

I've realized that when we give our wounds a voice we are able to move out of a space that keeps us locked in intense battle. The pain from my little wounded girl no longer has a tight grip on me because I listened, and finally believed her.

For me, animals have been a beautiful channel to understanding myself at a depth I could have never imagined. They opened me to a world of oracles and an even greater appreciation of how the invisible realm holds an incredible amount of wisdom for us which manifests itself in our outer world to help guide us.

As I was completing the final words for this chapter, another sign was presented to me. A friend on Facebook shared a quote on her wall that I'd shared before. When I clicked on the image, I saw the date I had originally posted it: March 2015.

The quote is by animal communicator Marta Williams and reads: *"Everything that throws us off throws our animals off. Our animals experience our imbalances as if the imbalances were their own. In acting out, all they really want to do is heal everything and everyone, so that there is peace and happiness."*

This speaks to what I believe about why animals share this earth with us. They are here as some of our greatest allies, guiding us to heal the wounds within us. Little did I know six years ago when I set the intention to open myself to the teachings of all animals that my love and respect for them would deepen in the ways it has.

Snake helped me to shed layers of what I no longer needed.

Laiola the white wolf encouraged me to keep my heart open.

Ollie the horse empowered me to trust myself and stand in my strengths.

And Gidget, my wise Buddha, was a steadfast reflection that helped me dig deep down into the darkness of my wounded child and finally rise into the light of my worthiness.

So for me, this isn't closure. But rather, a grateful and expanded soul that continues to evolve into the next phase of my journey.

With each step forward, I know: I'm fine just the way I am.

AFTERWORD

WHILE IN THE process of incorporating feedback from a beta reader into this manuscript, I decided to revisit a February 2018 journal entry in which I wrote about a dream. I shared part of that dream in Chapter 30.

As I read through the dream again, I gained some additional insight that I think is key to share. For some reason I thought I only saw dried blood in the tire tracks *after* I saw the dead dog lying in the road. Reading the entry again, I realized there were fresh blood drops that *led up* to my seeing the dog that was deceased.

Toward the end of my dream the man in it catches up to Dawn and me. Before we can speed off in her red car, he demands to know what the book is in the back of her car. I can't see the name of it because there is a sticky note covering the title. Dawn speeds away. A few moments later as we are driving through a gate the man is there again, demanding to see the book. I reach behind me, grab the book, and throw it at him as we speed away.

As I reflected again on this dream and all that had transpired since then, I was reminded that it was two days *after* the dream that I had the animal reading with Dawn, when the first thing Gidget shared was, "I'm Fine Just the Way I Am."

During the conversation Dawn said to me, "Perhaps you will write a book about all of this someday." Just two weeks before I'd had that same thought of writing a book about what I was going through, even though I was still struggling with the meaning of it. I had tucked the idea away to revisit at a later date.

I remember how Dawn said that perhaps a great title would be, *I'm Fine Just the Way I Am.*

I realize now that the dream spoke of this book you now hold in your hands. The title of the book was covered in the dream on February 24, but had been revealed to me at the time of the reading on February 26. I realize now that writing this book and sharing my story would be my way of "throwing the book" at the man who hurt me, though I do want to say again that I have forgiven this man. That act of forgiveness has been instrumental in my healing and in freeing myself of the burden that had weighed me down for decades.

When I shared this additional insight with Tayria, she offered this suggestion regarding the fresh blood spots I recently recalled in the dream. She said it would suggest that the wound was still actively bleeding at the time and wasn't yet healed over. And now it was. This made perfect sense to me.

I've definitely come a long way and also realize there are many layers to healing. Being open to this is important and helps us to not live in a space of fear.

One of those layers revealed itself the Monday before Mother's Day. Just when I thought I'd worked through the realization that I had not, as I'd long believed, made a conscious choice not to have children, but had instead been reacting to the childhood wound I'd suffered and then buried, I found myself feeling this pain at a new depth.

As I moved through my yoga practice that morning, some raw emotions bubbled to the surface. It felt as if for the very first time I was feeling at my core this deeply agonizing grief that I would never have children in this lifetime.

It was intensely painful to realize that had I'd not been wounded as a child I would have wanted to give birth to a child of my own. I would have loved a little girl. My tears were mixed with a rage that still needed to be processed, along with a deep sadness that overcame me.

Lying on my yoga mat I let all the emotions wash through me. I wept for the little girl I'd never know and rejoiced in the little girl I'd found. When the tears subsided I heard myself say out loud to those that didn't understand why I never had children: "This is why. This is why I didn't have kids."

It was a cathartic release.

That Friday I drove to my chiropractic appointment with Dr. Cindy. Every year on Mother's Day she and her staff present the patients who are moms with a flower in recognition of their role. Dr. Cindy has always given me a flower in appreciation of my role as a caretaker of special needs dogs, along with the human lives I've touched. It has always meant so much to me.

Little did I know how that flower would play out as a symbolic gesture of love and another letting go that would happen within the next twenty-four hours.

Early Saturday morning, the day before Mother's Day, I'd find myself sitting with Gidget in the veterinarian's office. Something wasn't right with Gidget's breathing. I could feel and see that her heart was beating hard in her chest. I also noticed she was breathing from her abdomen.

I had a gut sense about what was happening but I was too afraid to express it out loud.

I told Dr. Carrie what I had observed with Gidget, then she put her stethoscope to Gidget's heart and listened. A few moments later she said, "All four chambers of Gidget's heart are full of fluid."

I had noted over the past few months that Gidget was slowing down, but it wasn't anything I felt was out of the ordinary. Now I was sitting in the exam room, trying to digest the news that she had congestive heart failure.

Suddenly, I found myself panicking as I realized I was once again faced with deciding what was right for Gidget. Thankfully, I was able to reach Dawn by phone and tell her what was happening.

At one point I cried out to her, "I don't know how I'm going to live my life without Gidget!"

It struck me that just over a year ago I had thought I wanted to let Gidget go, and the months I'd spent feeling guilty about how narrowly I avoided that tragic mistake. And now here I was with the realization that it was likely time to say goodbye.

Dawn said, "This isn't about your fear, Barb, but about what Gidget wants."

After I weighed out all the options with careful consideration, I knew in my heart what the right decision was. Despite my pain, I was also able to feel immense gratitude for the opportunity to experience a deepening of love for Gidget, and our relationship, over the past year.

I gently stroked Gidget's back and the top of her sweet head, expressing to her my depth of love for her—thanking her for being my friend—and for her devotion and patience with me—especially in the last year as I learned to give voice to my personal childhood wounding. John, who had rushed to meet me at the clinic, sat beside us, caressing her and telling her what a good dog she was and that he loved her too.

After I made the humane decision to have her euthanized, I heard the chorus of the 1974 Terry Jacks song, *Seasons in the Sun*. I smiled through my tears. It was Gidget letting me know it was all okay no matter what. Afterall, despite our challenges, we had also had a great deal of joy and fun together.

To feel a precious life come to an end in one's arms cracks the heart wide open. The primal depth of sorrow I feel for her loss is something I felt no shame in expressing as I held her still body close to me.

As I slowly drove home, I realized that since 1984 we'd had a pet. There hasn't been a day in all those years that we didn't have at least one furry creature to come home to. Now I would find myself trying to acclimate to yet another unfamiliar space, but that was okay.

Still, as the days unfolded I felt so uncomfortable with the void I was feeling. I felt called to search for a book to support me and was led to *The Wild Edge of Sorrow* by Francis Weller. So much of what I read spoke eloquently to what I was experiencing. This passage in particular resonated:

For the most part, grief is not a problem to be solved, not a condition to be medicated, but a deep encounter with the essential experience of being human.

Though my heart ached terribly, I understood that I must feel the loss of Gidget deeply and completely. Just like she taught me last year to follow the signposts of a painful memory in order to heal, I had to do that now as I balanced my grief with the precious memories of life with her within each sacred moment.

The one thing that will stay with me forever, and one I hold the deepest gratitude for, is how Gidget held an incredible amount of patience and loving space for me.

It's the gift she gave me and one I must now give to myself.

It's time to care for me for a while now and spend more time with John. I've felt this coming for some time; I also have known for a long time that Gidget is the last special needs dog I will care for.

I've had to feel into this every step of the way and know that this is okay—even though what I'm experiencing has felt incredibly uncomfortable and lonely at times, along with this uncertainty that walks beside me.

Gidget helped me to see that feeling my way through it all is my best and truest compass. This is what will lead me as I continue to move forward. How do I ever thank her for that? By trusting this path she opened for me and following it with conscious allowing and curiosity.

Saturday afternoon, as we laid Gidget to rest in the garden outside my writing cottage, I remembered the flower Dr. Cindy had given me the day before. I ran into the house and took it out of the vase. I could feel my heart beating inside my chest as I walked back to the garden. I gently placed the flower with Gidget as we said our final goodbye. Waves of sorrow were mixed with gratefulness.

My favorite photo of Gidget is this one below. It was taken during a photoshoot for the cover of this book.

The last summer with her, and the one that followed the months working with the deep pain of my wounded childhood, was one of the best. As my love for Gidget deepened our relationship moved to a whole new level of understanding and love for each other.

I remember how at times I'd witness her sitting on the deck, soaking up the sunshine, and how she looked different to me—in a good and beautiful way.

And now, as I have softened into a more peaceful place since her passing, I realize why I love this photo so much.

It is her higher self I see, that wise Buddha dog I began to experience when she first came to live with us. This *is* the essence of who she was in life and in death. And it is the gift she left me with as a beautiful reflection to continue to live from that space of my own higher self too.

ACKNOWLEDGEMENTS

MY FIRST DEEP bow of gratitude goes to my dachshund, Gidget, also known as 'Buddha dog' because truly, she was the epitome of a wise one. Her steadfast devotion in walking this healing quest with me has been remarkable. I'm forever grateful to you sweet one.

To my husband, John, for loving me no matter what. My love for you has expanded ten-fold. While I've always felt blessed for our relationship, your presence in my life becomes more and more sacred every day.

To the woman who has held my heart from the beginning, my dear mama. For always believing in me and supporting me with your unconditional love, my heart rejoices in gratitude because of your love for me.

Animal communicator and good friend, Dawn Baumann Brunke, Spirit brought you into my life to stretch me far beyond what I could have ever imagined as you graciously held the most honest and loving space for me to evolve. Thank you from the bottom of my heart.

Joe Dwyer, animal chaplain and coach, for your commitment to all beings—human and animal, guiding us to live quality lives and in harmony with each other. Your gentle and compassionate nature was the medicine I needed to speak my truth even when it was difficult.

Tayria Ward, depth psychologist and dream analyzer for your exquisite work in listening to dreams. Your gentle and compassionate invitation to express the vision I held trapped within was the guiding light I needed to take the next imperative step to understanding it, releasing it, and finding my way home again to myself.

Thank you to my beta readers, Dawn Baumann Brunke, Pamela Kachelmeier, and Cynthia Morris, all of whom I have the deepest of respect and admiration for. Your support was stellar and your feedback was invaluable.

To my women's circle, Pam, Monica and Lisa, our souls were destined to come together for the greater whole and together, we have grown in immeasurable ways. Thank you for being you, so that I could feel free to be me.

To my editor, Dana Micheli, for taking my heartfelt words and working your special editorial magic to bring them to life in a new way while keeping my voice perfectly intact.

Friend and photographer, Lisa Lehmann, thank you for the photo used for the cover. You captured perfectly what I convey in words within my book.

To Matt Stone and his design team of 100 Covers for the cover design and interior layout design—such a seamless joint effort in working with you and your team, thank you!

Susan McCullen, thank you for graciously allowing me the use of the lyrics of your song, *You Can Relax Now*. A song I return to time and again as it always provides my heart such comfort.

As always, to my family and friends, thank you for your love and support.

Lastly, to the animals we share this planet with. Your wisdom and guidance continues to inspire me to expand my perspective and the importance of living in harmony with myself and with all beings.

RESOURCES

Animal Communication: Dawn Baumann Brunke, www.animalvoices.net
Animal Chaplain and Life Coach: Joe Dwyer, www.noblestrength.life
Dream Analysis and Depth Psychology: Tayria Ward, Ph.D., www.tayriaward.com
Equine Assisted Coaching, Pam Kachelmeier, www.equineaca.com
SoulCollage®: Discover Your Wisdom, Change Your World™, www.soulcollage.com
Pet Caregiver Burden: Mary Beth Spitznagel, Ph.D., www.petcaregiverburden.com
Transformational Breath®: Dr. Judith Kravitz, www.transformationalbreath.com
EMDR® therapy (Eye Movement Desensitization and Reprocessing): www.emdr.com
Oracle School: Colette Baron-Reid, www.colettebaronreid.com
Wisdom of the Oracle: deck by Colette Baron-Reid
The Mystical Shaman Oracle: deck by Alberto Villoldo, Colette Baron-Reid, and Marcla Lobos

Connect with Me

Website—**barbaratechel.com**
Facebook—**facebook.com/joyfulpause**
Instagram—**Instagram.com/barbtechel**

ABOUT THE AUTHOR

AS AN AUTHOR, oracle reader and intuitive guide, Barbara Techel gently guides women on inward quests to embrace and nurture a loving relationship of Self and live a more balanced, gracious and peaceful life.

She has been walking her own self-loving and transformational expedition since 2004. She's learned to discern and appreciate challenging times as opportunities to explore the deeper self, embrace what needs healing and emerge into feeling more peaceful and whole.

She has been interviewed on numerous radio stations and podcasts, appeared on TV for her books and her writing cottage, and featured in many magazines including *Woman's World*. She is the author of *Through Frankie's Eyes: One woman's journey to her authentic self, and the dog on wheels who led the way* and *Wisdom Found in the Pause—Joie's Gift*, plus two children's books, *Frankie the Walk 'N Roll Dog* and *Frankie the Walk 'N Roll Therapy Dog Visits Libby's House*.

To learn more about Barbara and her offerings,
visit www.barbaratechel.com